PLAN OF
THE
ENTRENCHED POSITION
OF THE
BRITISH GARRISON
AT
LUCKNOW.
1857.

IRON BRIDGE

Road from the Muchee Bhowun

R I V E R

Mosque

Mosque

Innis Garrison

Redan Bat.ty

Church Gar.n

RESIDENCY

Sheep Pen

Banglon Ho.

Oumand.n Garrison

5

4

Cubbius Garrison

Cubbius Battery

Published by Smith, Elder & Co. Cornhill, London 1858.

DIL-A-RAM KOTHIE

G O O M T E E

Captan Bazar

TAREE KHOTIE

FURRA BUX PALACE

CHUTTUR

MUNZIL

PALACE

Body Guard

Hospital

Un Barrac's Garrison

Financial Garrison

Begum Kottee Garrison

Post Office

Sages Garrison

Garrison

Square

Seikh Square

Seikh Square

Johannes Ho.

Mosque

Clock T.

JAIL

PYNE BAGH

Phillips Ho.

Mosque

References.

Line of defences shewn by a thick line   thus

Guns

Mortars

Nos 4 & 5 are unfinished Batteries

THE

DEFENCE OF LUCKNOW.

A DIARY

RECORDING THE DAILY EVENTS DURING THE SIEGE OF THE
EUROPEAN RESIDENCY

FROM 31ST MAY TO 25TH SEPTEMBER, 1857.

BY A STAFF OFFICER.

WITH A PLAN OF THE RESIDENCY.

The Naval & Military Press Ltd

published in association with

FIREPOWER
The Royal Artillery Museum
Woolwich

Published by
The Naval & Military Press Ltd
Unit 10 Ridgewood Industrial Park,
Uckfield, East Sussex,
TN22 5QE England
Tel: +44 (0) 1825 749494
Fax: +44 (0) 1825 765701
www.naval-military-press.com

in association with

FIREPOWER
The Royal Artillery Museum, Woolwich
www.firepower.org.uk

The Naval & Military Press

MILITARY HISTORY AT YOUR
FINGER TIPS

... a unique and expanding series of reference works

Working in collaboration with the foremost
regiments and institutions, as well as acknowledged
experts in their field, N&MP have assembled a
formidable array of titles including technologically
advanced CD-ROMs and facsimile reprints of
impossible-to-find rarities.

*In reprinting in facsimile from the original, any imperfections are inevitably
reproduced and the quality may fall short of modern type and cartographic standards.*

ADVERTISEMENT.

THE AUTHOR of this work desiring, for military reasons, to withhold his name from the publication, the Publishers feel it due to the public to vouch for the authenticity of the " Diary," by stating that the Author is an officer of the Staff of the Anglo-Indian Army, and was in Lucknow during the whole of the siege ; as, indeed, will be apparent from the full details of all that transpired in the garrison.

They beg to add that the only alteration made by them is the substitution of the most recent and complete list of the killed and wounded during

the defence, as given in the " Homeward Mail,"
for the list appended to the MS.   They have also
appended the eloquent despatch of Brigadier Inglis,
recording the services of the garrison.

65, CORNHILL:
　　Feb. 25th, 1858.

DIARY

OF

EVENTS AT LUCKNOW.

For about ten days previous to the outbreak, daily reports were made that an *émeute* was intended, and Sir H. M. Lawrence had ordered all kinds of stores to be purchased and stored in the "Muchee Bhawun" and the City Residency. But latterly the intelligence began to excite less attention, as so many days had passed away which had been named for the outbreak. On the evening of the 30th May, however, a sepoy of the 13th Native Infantry, who had shortly before received a reward from Sir Henry Lawrence for having assisted in the capture of a spy, came to Captain Wilson of the 13th Native

B

Infantry, Assistant Adjutant-General, and said he
could not help reporting that there would be a
rising amongst the sepoy regiments, to be commenced in the lines of the 71st Native Infantry that
evening at about 8 or 9 P.M.; but he was not certain at what hour. His manner in giving this information was *earnest* and *impressive*.

On that evening everything went on as usual;
all remained quiet in the cantonments, where Sir
Henry Lawrence was residing. Some days previously the ladies and children had been removed
to the Residency in the city, which place had
already been occupied by a party of the 32nd Foot
and two guns. The 9 P.M. gun was fired, and was
evidently the preconcerted signal for the mutiny;
for a few minutes after, whilst Sir Henry Lawrence
and his staff were at dinner at the Residency, a
sepoy came running in and reported a disturbance
in the lines. Two shots were heard in the 71st
lines. The horses of the staff were at once ordered,
and they proceeded to the lines. On the way, more
dropping shots were heard from the left of the 71st
lines. The party arrived in the camp, where about

300 men of Her Majesty's 32nd, with four guns of
Major Haye's battery, and two guns of the Oude
Irregular Force were posted, and found them all on
the alert. These were posted in a position on the
extreme right of the 71st lines (the whole front of
which they swept), and they were also contiguous to
the road leading from cantonments to the city.

Sir Henry Lawrence immediately took two guns
and a company of the 32nd with him on the road
leading to the town, and there took post; thereby
blocking up the road, and effectually cutting off all
access to the city. He sent back soon after for re-inforcements of the Europeans and for two more guns.
In the meantime, the officers of the several regiments had proceeded at once to their respective
lines. Bands of insurgents had meanwhile made
their way amongst the officers' bungalows, keeping
up as they went a desultory fire, which prevented
many from passing the roads towards the lines.
One of the first of these parties made straight for
the mess house of the 71st Native Infantry, whence
the officers had escaped but a few minutes before.
They exhibited great bloodthirstiness, making every

search for the officers, and ending by firing the
house. On several shots being fired from the
71st lines on the 32nd Foot and guns, the order
was given to open with grape; on which a rush was
made by the sepoys to the rear; when they passed
the infantry picket, which is situate in the centre of
cantonments. The picket was under the command
of Lieutenant Grant of the 71st Native Infantry.
His men remained with him till the mutineers were
close upon him. They then broke; but the subadar
of the guard, and some men of the 13th and 48th
Regiments, composing the guard, tried to save him
by placing him under a bed. A man of the 71st
Native Infantry, who was on guard with him, however, discovered the place of his concealment to the
mutineers, and he was there brutally murdered —
receiving no less than fifteen bayonet wounds,
besides some from musket balls.

From the first, Lieutenant Hardinge, taking with
him some few sowars of his Irregular Cavalry,
patrolled up and down the main street of the cantonments, and went to the officers' messes on the chance
of saving any lives. In the compound of the 71st

mess, he was fired at by a mutineer, who then rushed
upon him with his bayonet, which pierced his arm.
More than once the cantonments were thus patrolled
by Lieutenant Hardinge under a smart fire, with
the same humane intentions; but not in sufficient
force to prevent the burning and plundering of the
officers' bungalows, and of the bazaars. The excitement in the lines continued; while the 32nd remained quietly in position, awaiting the advent of
the remnants of the regiments who had remained
true to their colours. A remnant of the 13th Native
Infantry, about 200 men, with colours and treasure,
came up; and, according to previous arrangement,
joined and fell in on the right of the 32nd. A small
portion of the 71st, without being able to save their
colours or their treasure, (through the disaffection of
the native officer on duty,) also came up and took
post next the 32nd Foot. Of the 48th, nothing was
heard till 10 A. M. next day. About 10 o'clock P.M.
many of the mutineers had made their way up to
some empty artillery lines, outside the 71st Native
Infantry lines, whence they commenced firing.
Brigadier Handscomb, who had come up from the

rear of the 71st lines, was killed by a stray shot from this place : just as he had reached the left flank of the 32nd, he fell dead off his horse. The bungalows throughout the cantonments were most of them on fire. No attempt was subsequently made to attack the position. To secure the Residency bungalow, and that portion of the cantonment next the city road, 4 guns and a company and a half were taken up to the cantonment Residency, and the guns placed at each gate. All was now quiet, and the remainder of the night passed away without any further event. Nothing had been seen or heard of the 48th Native Infantry. Many officers had most wonderful escapes from death. Lieutenant and Adjutant Chambers of the 13th Native Infantry, was severely wounded in the leg, whilst effecting his escape from the magazine where he had taken a guard of his regiment.

May 31*st.* — At daylight, the force, consisting of some companies of Her Majesty's 32nd Foot, and the remnants of the native regiments, about 100 men 71st, and 220 men 13th Native Infantry, with part of the 7th Cavalry, and four guns, advanced down the parade in front of the lines of the several regiments. From the lines of the 13th Native Infantry about fifty men came, and said they had saved the magazine of that regiment. Hearing that the body of the rebels had retired towards the race course, where they had plundered the lines of the 7th Cavalry, and murdered Cornet Raleigh of that regiment (who had been left there sick) the whole force of cavalry and infantry, with four guns, proceeded thither, leaving Colonel Case with a portion of the 32nd in position in cantonments. On arriving in the open plain, a body of about 1200 men were seen in line in the distance, drawn up to the race course. Many of the cavalry galloped over at once to the insurgents. The guns then opened with round shot, which dispersed them, and they made the best of their way across country, followed immediately by the cavalry and guns, and, at a greater distance by the infantry. No opportunity offered for the guns to again open, owing to the celerity of their flight; but the cavalry hovered round and took about sixty prisoners, who were

brought into cantonments. The pursuit continued
in the same order until the guns were stopped by a
nullah, over which they could not cross. The
cavalry, however, continued their pursuit, and kept
it up for some ten miles. By 10 A.M. the force had
returned to cantonments, as the heat was excessive.

As most of the bungalows were burned (the
officers having lost everything) the troops were
moved into camp,—the 32nd and guns into the position they held formerly; the native regiments next
them on the right, and in the following order:—
13th next the 32nd, the 71st next, then the 48th,
with the 7th Cavalry on the extreme right. The
usual guards were kept by the native regiments,
and the cantonments regularly occupied. Owing to
this, the neighbouring country seemed to be re-
assured. Supplies came in regularly, and in plenty.
The exertions of all were redoubled to complete the
defences, and collect stores and supplies in Muchee
Bhawun and the city Residency. The former post,
originally occupied by the dependants of the late
king, had been selected by Sir Henry Lawrence as
a fitting place of security and retreat, in case matters

took an unfavourable turn. On the 16th of May, immediately on the receipt of intelligence from Meerut of the commencement of the outbreak, this stronghold, then in a very dilapidated condition, was occupied by the light company of the 13th and some guns, and measures were taken for its thorough cleansing. Supplies continued to be brought in and stored.

On the evening of the day on which the troops returned from the pursuit of the rebels, an insurrection took place in the city towards Hosainabad; the standard of the prophet was raised, and other means of religious persuasion used to excite the populace. The police of the city, under the energetic superintendence of Captain Carnegie, behaved well, and the movement was at once quelled, and the standard taken. News of the *émeute* at this place had by this time reached the district, and the rising of the neighbouring stations was to be looked for.

On the afternoon of the 4th June, parties of ladies and officers of the 41st Native Infantry, escorted by about twenty-five men of the regiment, who had remained faithful, came in, bringing the

news of the mutiny at Seetapore, and of the deaths
of Lieutenant-Colonel Birch, commanding the
regiment there, of Mr. Christian, and of other
civilians and ladies.   On the 5th, news came of the
mutiny at Cawnpore, but no particulars.   Reports
of all kinds were rife among the Bazaars; but no
authentic intelligence could be procured, as the
telegraph wire was cut.   From Benares the news
came in of the 37th Native Infantry having mutinied, and of their having been overpowered by
the rest of the force there.   But nothing further
transpired, for from that day to the 10th instant,
the communication was *in toto* interrupted.

June 10*th.*—The defences at the city Residency,
as well as the Muchee Bhawun, were increased,
and houses and buildings around them began at
once to be demolished.   Large stacks of firewood
were made, and houses and tents set apart for the
occupation of the European refugees, who were
arriving from the districts daily.   Provisions of all
sorts continued to be stored, including 110 hogs-
heads of beer just arrived from Cawnpore.

Besides the two important posts noted above, the range of buildings towards the Hosainabad quarter of the town were occupied by 2000 police under the direction of Captain Carnegie; a thousand more were ordered to be raised, and officers of the 41st were put in command of each of the police battalions. This day we heard, by native report, that General Wheeler was defending himself in the entrenchments at Cawnpore; but no letter was received.

June 11*th.*—Early this morning a false alarm was brought in from the Cawnpore road, that the enemy was upon us. Captain Evans, who had been sent out to gain information, returned with the above report, which created for a short period some needless alarm. We continued hard at work getting in supplies and adding to our defences. Many vague reports of disturbances were in circulation to-day.

June 12*th.* — On this day an instance of disaffection from within the camp occurred. The regiment of military police, commanded by Captain

Orr, mutinied in a body, rushed to their lines, seized their arms, and then set off in the direction of Cawnpore, giving themselves no time to inflict any damage in their quarter of the city. So great was their haste, that they failed to empty their own barracks, and left behind them their clothes and baggage. Information of this was given to head quarters; on which two guns of Major Kaye's battery, two companies of Her Majesty's 32nd, and some seventy Seikhs of the 1st Oude Irregular Cavalry, the whole under the command of Colonel Inglis, were despatched after them. They were pursued for some eight miles before they were come up with, and it was only by pushing on the cavalry and guns, without waiting for the slower movements of the infantry, that they were overtaken at all.

The guns opened fire as soon as practicable; they had come up well over some difficult ground, but their horses were, in consequence, so done up, that there was some difficulty in taking up the most desirable position. Once the cavalry charged well, but neither the result of their charge, nor of the practice of the artillery, was such as might have been expected. The enemy's loss was not exactly ascertained, but it was supposed that they had some twenty killed, and ten prisoners were brought in. Of Captain Forbes's men, two Pathans were killed on the spot; and some others, including a gallant old native officer, wounded. Mr. Thornhill, of the civil service, charging with them, was also wounded. All this time the infantry were far behind, unable to get up. A village lay to the front, in which many of the insurgents had taken refuge. Colonel Inglis forbade its bombardment, as it would have entailed much injury to innocent villagers; and the evening was, by that time, so far advanced, that the measure would probably not have sufficed to dislodge the mutineers.

About an hour remained to sunset; the guns and cavalry were a long way from the infantry, and many miles further from home. A return movement was therefore ordered, and accomplished successfully: the whole force returned about 8 o'clock, having gone over some sixteen or eighteen miles of ground.

The Europeans had marched well to the front.

It was a hard day's work for them, and two men were lost from apoplexy, for the heat was dreadful.

On this day the horses of the men of the 7th Cavalry were brought down and picketed close to the Baillie Guard ; as, with a very few exceptions, the 13th, 48th, and 71st Regiments of Native Infantry and 7th Cavalry had been ordered to proceed on leave till October, and their arms and accoutrements were brought down and deposited in the Residency.   (Vide No. 1 in the Appendix.)

June 13*th.*—Shot and shell both brought down to the garrison from Muchee Bhawun (about three-quarters of a mile).   Unabated exertions to add to the defences of the garrison.

The 13th Regiment of Native Infantry, 170 rank and file, came down from cantonments and encamped in the Residency compound.   Ineffectual efforts to blow down the *Furrahd Buksh* Gateway.   Three or four cases of cholera occurred at Fort Muchee Bhawun.   Officers' servants began to desert.   Intelligence was received from Fyzabad of the mutiny of all the troops there.   Heat beyond endurance.

Garrison in good spirits, and much elated at the brush after the Police Corps. Little reliance was placed in natives, and every possible precaution was taken to prevent any treachery. The native gunners, both in the Residency and at the Muchee Bhawun, were so posted as to be under the immediate fire of the Europeans, who watched them carefully both day and night. An officer was on duty at the gate all day long, to observe all incomers, and to prevent arms being brought in by others than those who had received passes.

June 14th. — Supplies of shot and shell brought in from Muchee Bhawun. Every exertion made to increase the defences of the garrisons. No reliable intelligence was procurable of the state of affairs at Cawnpore. Many idle rumours afloat, but not corroborated, with regard to a reinforcement of Europeans having arrived at that station from the north-west. Heat excessive. Several cases of cholera and smallpox. A few cases of the former disease proved fatal in Muchee Bhawun.

Hardinge's corps still steady. About 200 of the Oude Irregular Cavalry deserted last night.

June 15th. — A hundred barrels of gunpowder brought from the Muchee Bhawun, and buried in the Residency enclosure. Shot and shell continued to be brought into garrison from Muchee Bhawun. Uncovenanted servants were drilled with muskets. A tragic event occurred this day : — Serjeant-major K., 7th Light Cavalry, shot with a pistol, Riding-master Edridge, 7th Light Cavalry, in the heat of an argument. The riding-master died a few hours after. No reliable intelligence was procured from Cawnpore, though vague reports were in circulation. The death of Lieutenant Colonel Fisher, commanding 15th Irregular Cavalry, by the hands of his own men, was reported.

Captain Gall's servant returned to the garrison this day, reporting his master's death, which took place by stratagem, and by the hands of his own men. Captain Gall was proceeding in disguise *en route* to Allahabad, with twelve sowars of his own corps, and had proceeded about fifty miles on his way, when his murder took place. All officers of the cantonments were ordered down to the garrison, with the exception of the commanding officers and regimental staff. Twenty-three lacs of rupees were buried close in front of the Residency, for security, and to avoid the necessity of guards and sentries over it. Rum and porter (one-half) was received into the Residency from Muchee Bhawun. Fever was prevalent. The Seikhs of the 13th Native Infantry, numbering about fifty men, were formed, at their own request, into a company, under the command of Captain Germon, and sent to Muchee Bhawun. Spare clothing of the 13th was brought in from cantonments. Continued efforts were made to blow up the Furrah Buksh Gate. The flooring of the first story fell in this day.

June 16th.—A quantity of shot and shells came in from Muchee Bhawun; also an 18-pounder gun. The shot was piled, as far as possible. On this date, there were seven 18-pounders in position. The whole day was expended in working hard at a battery in a position commanding the Cawnpore-road, and in unroofing

houses, burying powder, &c.   The gate leading into
the Furrah Buksh came down in the course of
the forenoon with a great crash, after many futile
attempts had been made for its destruction.   This
was an important point gained, as the Residency compound was quite commanded from the top of this
gate.

This morning, twenty-two conspirators, emis-
saries from Benares and elsewhere, who had been
sent to corrupt the troops at this place, were captured
in a house in the centre of the city.   Information
having been given to Captain Hughes, commanding
the 4th Irregular Infantry, he directed two staunch
native officers to put themselves on the watch, and
to pretend participation in the disaffection.   This
they did, and by this means, with Captain Carnegie's
assistance, Captain Hughes was enabled to effect the
capture of these inciters to mutiny.   They were
forthwith brought to a drum-head court-martial
and the whole of them condemned to death.

June 17th.—This morning, four of the men sen-
tenced yesterday, were hanged at the Muchee

Bhawun ; the remaining eighteen were liberated, as some doubts were entertained of their guilt.

Vague and most contradictory rumours came in this day about Cawnpore, but no authentic intelligence could be gained. The intelligence department, under the supervision of Mr. Gubbins, with two assistants, seemed to experience great difficulty in procuring reliable intelligence. Amongst others, Colonel Palmer, commanding the 48th Regiment Native Infantry, came in from the cantonments, waited on the Brigadier-General, and reported large assemblies of men near cantonments, the immediate abandonment of which he most earnestly advocated.

Although there yet remained some twenty-five lacs in the treasury, the expenditure had been on such an enormous scale during the last week, that cash payments were suspended, unless in exceptional cases. The money rewards, &c., promised to men of the several infantry regiments, whose good behaviour had been conspicuous on the night of the mutiny, were discharged by promissory notes. Major Apthorp of the 41st Native Infantry had an advance made to him to pay up and discharge twenty-five of his men who had escorted in the officers and ladies from

Seetapore; as it was reported by one of his drummers, that even these faithful few, who had all been
promised promotion by Sir Henry Lawrence for
their fidelity on that occasion, had expressed themselves to the effect that if Rajah Maun Singh came
against them, they would all have to go over, and
would murder their officers.

June 18*th.* — The force at the Residency, consisting of the regular troops, civilians, volunteers of all
sorts, and, in fact, every man within the defences
not incapacitated by sickness, were ordered by Sir
Henry Lawrence to parade at sunrise. Every man
was to be at the post he was to occupy in case of an
attack; and those to whom no posts had been assigned mustered in front of the Residency, for the
purpose of having a post or duty assigned them.
The Brigadier-General inspected the whole of them,
and visited all the outposts and picquets.

In the evening of the same day the force was
paraded a second time, and minutely inspected by
Colonel Inglis. A body of fifty volunteers, belonging to the several offices, had been trained and

drilled to use firearms. To them was entrusted the defence of two outposts near the Post-office, which place had been made a very strong position. The officers comprising the volunteer corps of cavalry were also given arms, to be able to make a stand and defend themselves within their own quarters. They furnished sentries at night, and exercised a supervision over some seventy Seikh sowars, the remains of the Oude Irregular Cavalry. These, as well as the body of clerks, &c., mentioned above, were in all respects armed and accoutred like private soldiers. Besides this, many of the volunteers and officers were instructed in gun drill; and, at the Muchee Bhawun, by Sir Henry's directions, some fifty or sixty of the 32nd Foot were told off for the same work. A very strong battery (the Redan) was commenced this day; it completely commanded the iron bridge and the road leading to cantonments.

The servants of Captains Staples, 7th Cavalry, and Burmester, 48th Native Infantry, returned and reported the murder of those officers whose heads, they stated, were carried to the Nana at Cawnpore; and that Lieutenant Boulton, of the

7th Cavalry, jumped his horse into the river, and nothing further had been heard of him. Owing to the want of rain, the heat had now become intense. Cholera and dysentery were on the increase; chiefly at the Muchee Bhawun.

Reports came in of some bodies of the enemy being at a place called Nawab Gunge, about eighteen miles from Lucknow, and Captain Forbes, with twenty Sikhs and ten of the volunteer cavalry corps, was sent out there to ascertain the presence or otherwise of the enemy. They returned in the evening bringing information that there was no one. The company of the 10th Oude Irregular Force was brought down from the Dâk Bungalow to the jail. This regiment was the last to give way at Seetapore, and it was reported they did not molest their officers.

Quantities of bhoosa were collected and stored within the Racket Court, which was now half full.

June 19th. — This morning Sir Henry Lawrence inspected the Muchee Bhawun minutely. More small arm ammunition was brought in from thence to the Residency.

A fresh case of small pox occurred to day (Mr. Bird, who was immediately removed to a tent in the compound). The uncovenanted volunteers were again minutely inspected this afternoon. The engineer officers were very hard at work completing the batteries and defences. Upwards of 3000 coolies were at work unroofing houses in the vicinity of our defences.

From cantonments all the spare baggage, &c. was brought in, and every preparation made to prevent confusion in case the position there should be abandoned. In the city of Lucknow everything remained perfectly quiet,—the administration of justice was in no way impeded. Grain was stored in large quantities in the church.

June 20*th.*—This day, "the Redan" was completed. It consisted of one 18-pounder gun and one 9-pounder, with two mortars in their rear—the whole commanding the iron bridge and open country across the river. The Cawnpore 18-pounder battery was very nearly finished, and an expense magazine establishment near it.

A letter bearing date the 18th instant was received from Cawnpore, written by Captain Moore
of Her Majesty's 32nd Foot, by direction of General Wheeler,—it informed us, at last, of occurrences at that place. All the numerous previous
reports regarding the reinforcements of European
troops said to have been received, were thereby
falsified. No such reinforcements had ever been
received. The letter informed us of their ability
to hold out for some fifteen days more. The dreadful news of a boat load of European ladies, women,
and children, from Futteghurh, having been intercepted at Cawnpore and assassinated there, was
confirmed by natives.

Supplies continued to be stored, but they were
collected with difficulty and at increased prices.

Large stacks of firewood, which had been stored
in case of difficulties, were regularly arranged in a
semicircle, protecting the front of the Residency, and
covered with earth; these formed an embankment
six feet in height, and embrasures were cut through
them for the guns, of which there were four 9-
pounders on that side.

June 21st.—Two hundred guns, many of large calibre, were found in the gardens of the Seish Mahul, behind the Dowlut Khana (a large building on the north side of the city). There were no carriages to them. This startling discovery was luckily made in time. Twenty-seven guns were at once brought in, and arrangements made for parking the remainder.

In the evening, as the church was full of grain, divine service was performed in Mr. Gubbins's garden; and, during the night, Sir Henry himself once more visited the outposts, which had, by this time, been brought to a satisfactory state. The guards of the uncovenanted service were well on the alert, and prepared for any emergency. The difficulty of procuring all kinds of grain daily increased. Many rumours of a strong force marching on Lucknow from Fyzabad. The force in cantonments held in readiness to march at one hour's notice, to the Residency and the Muchee Bhawun.

June 22nd.— This morning Captain Radcliffe's troop of volunteer cavalry were despatched, at 1 A. M.,

towards Nawab Gunge, to patrol the roads in that
direction, in conjunction with the Seikhs, in order to
gather information.   About 4 o'clock A. M. a thunderstorm from the east, with the much wished for rain,
came on.   It lasted no very long time, and afforded
only a temporary relief from the excessive heat.

Sir Henry Lawrence made an excursion as far
as the Husainabad Kotwallee, garrisoned by nearly
3000 police and others, and inspected them and
the defences of that place.   He also visited the
Dowlut Khana, an old magazine, and on his return
went over the Muchee Bhawun defences.   All our
available spare carts, hackeries, and wagons, were
to-day employed in bringing in the guns found
yesterday.   Many of them were of large size.   The
unroofing and clearing away of houses continued
without intermission, and every exertion was made
to remove anything which might afford cover in the
immediate vicinity of our defences.

June 23rd. — Two men executed this morning
at the Muchee Bhawun, — the one a mutineer
(a naick of the 71st Native Infantry), the other

a man who had, on the night of the mutiny,
threatened the life of Mr. Yarbury, a merchant.

A large battery traced out, looking to the west-
ward. It was to consist of at least two heavy guns,
and to be raised so as to bombard the town in that
direction. A considerable amount of labour would
have been required to raise it to the necessary
elevation. Altogether it was the most extensive
work of the kind we had yet undertaken. An
8-inch howitzer, which had been discovered with
the other guns at the Seesh Muhal, was mounted
and placed in the Redan battery.

Captain Radcliffe's troop of volunteers, numbering
forty sabres, were drilled and exercised daily; and
now that the majority of the Irregular Cavalry had
deserted, and the remainder were not considered
trustworthy, the troops supplied two mounted orderlies every morning to escort Sir Henry Lawrence
into the city.

The commanding officer of the 71st Regiment
Native Infantry reported the remnant of the Seikhs
of his regiment (about twenty men, who had remained
true on the night of the *émeute*) as being in an

insubordinate state, and no longer to be trusted.
Sir Henry Lawrence desired them to be sent to
him, and spoke to them.   They had asked for their
discharge before, and had very precipitately been
disarmed by their commanding officer, without sufficient authority.   After being spoken to by the
Brigadier-General, they professed themselves quite
willing to continue their services : they were taken
at their word, their arms restored, and were kept at
the Residency under the command of an officer.

A letter was received yesterday from Cawnpore,
written under the direction of General Sir H. M.
Wheeler, K.C.B., giving very bad news indeed.   It
stated that the enemy shelled them for the last eight
days, which had had fearful effect within their crowded
trenches, and one third of their number had been killed.

In the meantime, the Muchee Bhawun garrison
had not been idle at their defences, and Sir Henry
was constant in his visits there, as well as to the
Seesh Muhal, and Dowlut Khana.   On the west-
ward side of the Muchee Bhawun, a heavy tower
was commenced ; a work of great labour, from which
a flanking fire could be given.   In the vicinity of

the fort, as at the Residency, houses were unroofed, and walls pulled down, so as to leave as little shelter as we could. Magazines were constructed, and the powder placed in safety.

June 24th.—Heavy clouds, and every appearance of rain throughout the day, but none fell. Heat excessive. Sir Henry Lawrence proceeded at daybreak as usual, attended by his staff and two orderlies from the volunteer cavalry, and inspected the Dowlut Khana, Seesh Muhal, Imaumbarah Kolwallee, and Muchee Bhawun; and in the evening he proceeded five miles on the Fyzabad road, to ascertain if there was a good position we could take up, in case of an advance of the rebels in that direction.

The last of the guns discovered in the Seesh Muhal garden were brought in to-day. Four of them were of very large calibre — two being 32-pounders. *Native* reports describe the force at Cawnpore as being hard pressed. Native reports from Allahabad were good. Much progress made in knocking down and unroofing the houses in the *immediate* vicinity of the Muchee Bhawun and Resi-

dency. The Racket Court was now filled with
bhoosa for the cattle, and thatched in. We were
supposed to have nearly three months' supply of
provisions now stored. The mutineers were reported to have arrived at Nawabgunge (eighteen
miles distant), and were said to have with them
some sixteen guns.

June 25th.— The tower at the Muchee Bhawun
was carried on this day with great ardour. Crowds
of coolies were employed under the direction of Lieutenant Innes of the Engineers. This defence was to
command the stone bridge, the Imaumbara, and a
number of high mosques facing that side of the Muchee Bhawun. Elephants were yoked to one of the
heaviest guns,—luckily there was some gear for the
purpose, and the experiment turned out successful.

A native rumour reported the arrival of a strong
force of mutineers at Nawabgunge, where it was
said they were to remain till they had consolidated
their force. Good news came in to-day from Allahabad in a letter from the officer commanding
the 1st Madras Fusileers, dated the 18th of June, in

answer to one despatched from this place on the 15th instant. Colonel Neil's letter gave little or no detail, beyond stating that he assumed command of the fort on the 11th instant; that there had been much fighting, but all the mutineers were entirely broke and dispersed, and the cantonments reoccupied. Cholera broke out on the 18th among the Fusileers, who in two days had had amongst them 100 cases, forty of which had proved fatal. Every effort was being made to push on troops to Cawnpore, but the road was not open, and carriage was difficult to procure: also that Her Majesty's 84th were close at hand, and that the telegraphic communication had been re-established between Calcutta and Allahabad. No authentic intelligence from Cawnpore, and much anxiety was felt regarding the force there.

All appearance of rain had gone off, and the heat was almost insupportable. The river had risen about a foot and a half, and was no longer fordable. A letter was received from Mrs. Dorin, stating that she was residing in a hut close to Seetapore, soliciting money and assistance, and reporting the murder of her husband. Numbers of gun-barrels and locks were brought in from the old magazine, where a great quantity of crowsfeet were found, and ordered to be brought in to-morrow. Behind Mr. Ommanney's house, a very large battery was commenced by Lieutenant Hutchinson. Quantities of grass and stores were brought in.

June 26th. — This morning Sir Henry Lawrence, accompanied by his staff, as usual inspected the principal buildings in the vicinity of the Muchee Bhauwn and the new round tower, at which great progress had been made, and in which not less than 300 coolies were at work. Proceeding thence he inspected the newly completed defences opposite the Kolwallee. On his return, Sir H. Lawrence received a letter from Major Raikes at Mynpoorie, giving intelligence of the capture of the city of Delhi on the 13th instant (this afterwards turned out to be a false report). A royal salute was ordered to be fired from the Residency, Muchee Bhawun, and cantonments, and a *feu-de-joie* was fired by the Irregulars, who were quartered in the Dowlut Khana, under the command of

Brigadier Gray. Many useful stores, consisting of unwrought materials, rope, and platforms, were brought in from the old magazine. Considerable progress was made in a new battery for heavy guns, which had been commenced in the rear of Mr. Ommanney's house.

In the afternoon, a letter, dated June 23rd, was received from Colonel Neil, commanding at Allahabad, reporting all well there; that 750 Europeans had arrived, and that 1000 more would be with him on the next day; that every effort was being made to despatch 400 Europeans, two guns, and 300 Seikhs to Cawnpore, but that much difficulty was experienced in procuring carriage.

Also, at sunset, a letter was received from Sir H. M. Wheeler, K.C.B., dated the 24th instant, detailing his losses, and giving an account of the outbreak, and stating that he had supplies for only eight or ten days at the farthest. His letter was replied to at once, and he was informed by Sir Henry Lawrence of the news received from Allahabad, and also that in ten days at the farthest he would receive aid from Allahabad, and that he

c

must husband his resources as much as possible ;
that the force at Lucknow was threatened by an
attack from eight or ten regiments, three or four of
which were within twenty miles.

A reward of one lac of rupees was offered this day
for the capture, within a week, dead or alive, of the
Nana, at Cawnpore, and means were taken to have
the proclamation widely disseminated.   With the
larger battery commenced to the south, behind Mr.
Ommanney's house, we had three large batteries in
progress, and were also busily employed in destroying, as far as possible, any buildings that might give
cover in the vicinity.   Five or six elephants were
in course of training to drag heavy guns, so as to
enable us to move out without delay, should cir-
cumstances require a heavy gun to be taken out.

27th June. — This morning a letter from Lieutenant Burnes, Adjutant of the 10th Regiment
Oude Irregular Infantry, late at Seetapore, was
received.   It gave an account of the mutiny at that
place, and of the escape of himself, Sir M. Jackson,
Bart., and sisters (one of whom had been carried off

for some days by the sepoys and brought back), and some others, to a place called Mitowlee, where they claimed and received the protection (charily given) of a rajah: they were then all in the jungles, suffering the *greatest* hardships. It also mentioned the safety of another party with Captain Hearsey; who, however, were also in the jungles. Many of these seem to have had the most hair-breadth escapes. No rain had yet fallen, and the heat was most oppressive. The cholera had abated during the past few days, but several cases of small-pox had, however, occurred. The river was reported to have fallen a foot since yesterday.

A report was in circulation early in the day, that General Wheeler had made terms with " the Nana," at Cawnpore; but few believed it, and in the evening it was reported incorrect, as heavy firing had been heard yesterday at Cawnpore from Bunnee. Three boxes of crow's feet and a great number of musket-barrels and unwrought stores were brought in from the old magazine at the Dowlut-Khana; also a very large quantity of gun carriage-wheels. The force at Nawabgunge was

said to be increasing, but very undecided as to
what to do. A great force of coolies were at work,
and much progress was made in the defences at
Muchee Bhawun and the Residency.

28th June. — This morning, at about 3 A.M., we
had a heavy fall of rain, which continued with
slight intervals till 7 A.M.   Sir Henry Lawrence
proceeded to Hosainabad and examined the defen-
sive preparations made there; returning by the Muchee Bhawun, he found that the buildings occupied
by the 32nd had hardly leaked at all.   Divine
service was performed in the City Hospital (brigade mess), occupied by the officers of the 7th
Cavalry, 13th, 48th, and 71st Native Infantry, at
7 A.M.   Spies stated that the 17th Regiment Native
Infantry, numbering between 250 and 300 men, had
gone with five lacs of rupees to Onao on the Cawnpore road — it was believed with the intention of
proceeding to Cawnpore.

It having been reported that there were many
jewels and valuables in the king's palace, which
might fall into the hands of the mutineers, a party

under Major Banks, consisting of fifty of the 13th, twenty Seikhs 71st Native Infantry, and the European Volunteer Cavalry, were sent out to fetch them in; which they did about 6 P.M., and reported that they had discovered a large gun.

About 7 P.M. three different natives brought in the very sad and distressing news that the Cawnpore force, having no more ammunition left, had entered into a treaty with their enemies, after which they had all been treacherously murdered, as they embarked in boats to proceed down the river to Allahabad.

Mrs. Dorin, wife of Lieutenant Dorin, who lately commanded the 10th Regiment Oude Irregular Forces, arrived this evening in a country cart, disguised as a native, and accompanied by some clerks. She was for very many days secreted in a village close to Seetapore, and her escape is wonderful. The Serjeant-Major's wife of the 9th Regiment Oude Irregular Infantry also arrived in a doolie, severely wounded. From 8 to 10 o'clock P.M. it rained heavily. A letter, dated the 21st June, received from Benares from Mr. Gubbins, giving an account of the number of Europeans

coming up the country, and describing the state
of Benares and Allahabad ; reporting also an action
at Delhi on the 8th instant, when the British troops
captured twenty-six guns. News also received from
Agra by letter from Captain Nixon, political agent.

June 29th. — This morning, a brass gun, a 21-
pounder which had been accidentally discovered
yesterday by the party who had been despatched
under Major Banks, to bring in valuables from the
palace (called the " Kiser Bagh,") was brought in,
carriage and waggon all completely ready for immediate service. Some grape shot and powder,
chiefly damaged, was also discovered in an adjacent
house.

The people in charge of the palace, without
giving a thought to resistance as it was at first
expected they might do, nevertheless showed an
evident reluctance to give information where the
arms, &c. were stored. However, it came out at
last, that there were more arms within the palace,
and a party was despatched to secure them. Seven
cart-loads were brought in; chiefly flint muskets,

with a few spears, &c. : 4 small guns were also discovered and brought in.

A small party of volunteers, cavalry (twelve men
including officers), were sent along the Cawnpore road
to bring in information. After going some twelve
miles, they returned, having learnt that there were
some two or three regiments not far off them. Captain Forbes, with the Seikh Cavalry, was sent off at
sunrise to patrol the Nawabgunge road. Six men
were also sent on the Sultanpore road to gain information. Both the parties returned at sunset,
Captain Forbes bringing intelligence that the enemy
were at Chinât, nine miles off.

Our defences progressed, but labour was not so
easy to procure as it had been some days before.

*   *   *   *   *

The enemy being in strength so near, it was
deemed advisable to withdraw the troops from cantonments, which was quietly done at sunset; and it
being expected that the enemy would march on
Lucknow, Sir Henry Lawrence thought it advisable to move out with a strong force, hoping to
meet and oppose them before they entered the

suburbs of the city. In order to prevent any notice
reaching the enemy of the intended movement, the
orders were not given out publicly till 3 o'clock on
the following morning, and at the same hour twenty
Seikhs under Lieutenant Birch were to be sent to
the Iron Bridge, in order to prevent any one
crossing over with intelligence of the movement to
the enemy.

June 30*th.* — Pursuant to orders, a force, comprising 150 of the 32nd from the Muchee Bhawun, 130
of the 13th Native Infantry, forty Seikhs of the 13th
Native Infantry, the 48th, numbering fifty bayonets,
the European cavalry thirty-six strong, the Oude
Irregular Cavalry, about ninety men, four of the
guns of Kaye's battery (Europeans), two of
Alexander's guns (natives), two of Bryce's guns
(natives), and an eight-inch howitzer, found in the
town a few days ago, and which was drawn by two
elephants, assembled at the iron bridge at 5.45
A. M.   The advance guard was composed of twenty-
five Seikh Cavalry, and fifteen European Cavalry ;
twenty Seikh Infantry, and twenty of the 32nd Regi-

ment, the whole under the command of Captain Stevens of the 32nd Foot.

The eight-inch howitzer, two guns of Alexander's battery, two of Kaye's battery, the 13th Native Infantry, two of Bryce's guns, and the detachment of the 32nd Foot, formed the main body, and marched in the above order. The rear guard was composed of the 48th Native Infantry, under Colonel Palmer; the whole force being under the personal command of Sir Henry Lawrence. It was the Brigadier-General's original intention only to proceed to the end of the Pucka road, to the village of Kocaralee; and on their arrival there, our force was halted, and the Brigadier-General, with the advanced guard, proceeded about a mile to the front, whence no one was to be seen. The force was on the point of being ordered to return, when it was decided to make a further reconnaissance; and soon after the enemy were fallen in with, in overwhelming numbers, and the force was compelled to retire with the loss of the eight-inch howitzer, and three 9-pounders.

The enemy came boldly on, and invested us on all sides, firing from all the houses round, which they rapidly loopholed; they also erected a hasty battery for the eight-inch howitzer across the river, from which they threw several well-directed shells; and they began to collect boats for a bridge across the river, the iron bridge being under fire from the Redan.

July 1st. — The enemy threw in a very heavy fire of musketry all day and night. Early in the morning they advanced to attack, but were repulsed on all sides with considerable loss from our shells, guns, and musketry. Mr. McRae, of the Civil Engineers Department, and Lieutenant Dashwood, 48th Native Infantry, were wounded, while assisting in working an 18-pounder in the Post Office Battery.

During the day attempts were made to get messengers to cross over to the Muchee Bhawun fort; two or three men started, but as their success was very doubtful, it was determined to work the telegraph on the top of the Residency. This had been previously arranged by the engineer in concert with one on the Muchee Bhawun; it simply consisted of one post with a bar at the top, from which were suspended in one row black stuffed bags, each having its own pulley to work it. After having attracted the attention of the Muchee Bhawun Garrison, the greatest difficulty was found in working the telegraph, from various causes; the chief of which was the tremendous fire which the enemy opened on the spot directly they saw our people on the flat open roof of the Residency. It rained rifle balls, principally from the top of the jail, and some few of the ropes of the bags were actually cut by them; then the pulleys went wrong, and twice the whole machine had to be taken down, and after readjustment put up again. After three hours' hard work under a broiling sun and a heavy fire, the transfer of messages was at last completed.

The message was simply an order to blow up the place and come to the Residency at 12 P.M., bringing the treasure and guns, and destroying as much as possible all spare ammunition. The night was anxiously looked for, as the retreat of the retiring force might be intercepted, and the enemy had the advantage of position. To help the movement, the Brigadier-

General gave orders that shortly before 12 P.M., the
different mortars and guns from our batteries should
open fire, in order to distract the attention of the
enemy.   This was carried out; especially towards
the iron bridge, by which the force must pass.

The movement was most successfully performed;
and so quick and noiseless was the march, that at
12.15 the head of the column was at the Lower Water
Gate.   Here there was some little delay, as the force
not being so quickly expected, the gates had not been
opened.   A very serious accident had nearly happened in consequence of this, for the leading men,
finding the gates closed, shouted out " Open the
gates," and the artillerymen at the guns above,
which, loaded with grape, covered the entrance, mis-
took the words for " Open with grape," and were
already at the guns, when an officer put them right.
The whole force came in without a shot being fired.

The explosion had not yet taken place; but soon,
a shake of the earth, a volume of fire, a terrific report, and an immense mass of black smoke shooting
far up into the air, announced to Lucknow, that
240 barrels of gunpowder, and 594,000 rounds of

ball and gun ammunition, had completed the destruction of Muchee Bhawun, which we had with
so much labour provisioned and fortified.

July 2nd. — Arrangements were made for posting
and stationing the Muchee Bhawun force which
came in last night, and placing the field-pieces in
position; all of which Sir H. Lawrence himself
personally superintended.   About 8 A.M. Sir Henry
returned to the Residency, and, being much fatigued,
laid down on his bed.   Soon after an eight-inch shell
from the eight-inch howitzer of the enemy, entered
the room at the window, and exploding, a fragment
struck the Brigadier-General on the upper part of the
right thigh near the hip, inflicting a fearful wound.
Captain Wilson, who was standing alongside the bed
with one knee on it at the time, reading a memorandum to Sir Henry, was knocked down by falling
bricks and slightly wounded in the back by a piece
of shell.   Sir H. Lawrence's nephew, Mr. Lawrence,
had an equally narrow escape, being on another bed
close by: he was not hurt; the fourth individual in
the room was a native servant, who lost one of his

feet by a fragment of the shell. It was at once pro-
nounced that Sir Henry Lawrence's wound was
mortal, and his sufferings were great. He immediately sent for Major Banks, and appointed him to
succeed him as Chief-Commissioner, and appointed
Colonel Inglis to command the troops. He was then
removed to Dr. Fayrer's house, which was somewhat
less under fire. About noon this day, a round shot
came into a room on the lower story of the residency,
and shattered the thigh of Miss Palmer (daughter of
Colonel Palmer, 48th Regiment, Native Infantry)
so dreadfully, that instant amputation was obliged to
be resorted to. All the garrison were greatly grieved,
and the Natives much dispirited at our severe loss,
in that popular and very distinguished officer, Sir
Henry Lawrence.

A perfect hurricane of jinjal, round shot, and
musketry all day and all night. Probably not less
than 10,000 men fired into our position from the
surrounding houses; the balls fell in showers, and
hardly any place was safe from them. Many of
the garrison were hit in places which, before the
siege, it was considered would be perfectly safe;
but the enemy fired some of them from a great dis-

tance out of the town, from the tops of high houses, and the balls fell everywhere.

July 3rd.—It is difficult to chronicle the proceedings of these few days, for everywhere confusion reigned supreme. That unfortunate day of Chinât precipitated everything, inasmuch as we were closely shut up several days before anything of the kind was anticipated. People had made no arrangements for provisioning themselves: many indeed never dreamt of such a necessity ; and the few that had were generally too late. Again, many servants were shut out the first day, and all attempts to approach us were met by a never-ceasing fusilade. But though they could not get in, they succeeded in getting out; and after a few days, those who could boast of servants or attendants of any kind formed a very small and envied minority. The servants in many instances eased their masters of any superfluous article of value, easy of carriage. In fact, the confusion can be better imagined than described.

The head of the Commissariat had, most unfortunately for the garrison, received a severe wound at

Chinât, which effectually deprived them of his valuable aid. His office was all broken up; his goomastahs
and baboos were not with us, and the officers appointed
to assist him were all new hands. Besides all this,
the first stores opened were approachable only by
one of the most exposed roads, and very many of
the camp followers preferred going without food to
the chance of being shot. Some did not know
where to apply, so that for three or four days, many
went without rations; and this in no small degree
added to the number of desertions. Owing to these
desertions, the commissariat and battery bullocks
had no attendants to look after them, and went
wandering all over the place looking for food; they
tumbled into wells, were shot down in numbers by
the enemy, and added greatly to the labour which
fell on the garrison, as fatigue parties of civilians and
officers, after being in the defences all day repelling
the enemy's attack, were often employed six and
seven hours burying cattle killed during the day, and
which from the excessive heat became offensive in a
few hours. The artillery and other horses were
everywhere to be seen loose, fighting and tearing at

one another, driven mad for want of food and water; the garrison being too busily employed in the trenches to be able to secure them.

Poor Sir H. Lawrence suffered somewhat less to-day, but was sinking fast, and at times his mind wandered. A tremendous fire all day, more particularly on the Baillie Guard and Dr. Fayrer's house where Sir Henry was lying. We thus early in the siege learnt that all our proceedings inside were known (through some party or other) to our enemies. Miss Palmer died to-day, and Mr. Ommanney of the Civil Service, was dangerously wounded under the ear by a grape shot, while in the Redan battery.

July 4th. — A tremendous fire all night; but no effort was made to storm our position. To the great grief of our garrison, Sir Henry Lawrence died this morning about 8 o'clock, from the effects of his wound. Shortly before his death, Mr. G. H. Lawrence while standing in the front verandah of Dr. Fayrer's house, was wounded by a musket-ball through his right shoulder.

At night, there was a great uproar in the city,
which evidently underwent a thorough plundering.
Notwithstanding this, the same heavy fire was kept
up throughout the night. Every one at work trying
to throw up some shelter for himself. In the
course of the day, a 9-pounder, brought by the
insurgents and placed behind a small mosque close to
our furthest water-gate, was spiked by a private of
the 32nd and four others from Innes's post, who
shot four of the enemy. The enemy were taken by
surprise while at their dinner.

July 5th.—From 2 till 6 o'clock A.M., heavy
rain; and extremely heavy firing all day. Several
casualties among our garrison. A soldier of the
32nd was said to have killed five men in ten shots
from the Cawnpore battery, which was subjected
to a very severe musketry fire. Continued efforts
were made to collect all the horses and secure them,
but it was impossible to do anything during the day.
The fire was so heavy, and the night was so dark, it
was difficult to get hold of the animals, who were
half mad; added to which four or five horses were

killed daily, which had to be buried at night by parties of officers, who, after being exposed to a fearful sun in the trenches all day, were often out in the rain till 12 and 1 o'clock in the morning, engaged in burying horses and bullocks, in order to prevent the dreadful stench which would otherwise have been increased, and which had already become almost insupportable.

July 6th.—The usual amount of musketry and cannon fire all the morning: about 2 o'clock in the afternoon it became very severe, especially towards the Baillie Guard, which seemed the favourite point to-day for the heaviest fire. A heavy cannonade heard about three miles off for about half an hour. About 4 P.M. the flashes of the guns were distinctly seen. The cause was unknown. The enemy digging trenches in all directions. The carriage of one of our 9-pounders was disabled by the enemy.

July 7th.— A heavy fire all the morning.

A sortie was made by fifty of the 32nd and twenty Sikhs, led by Captain Lawrence, Captain Mansfield,

Ensign Green, 13th Native Infantry, and Ensign Studdy, — the latter led. The storming took place at noon. The object was to examine M. Johannes' house, and discover if the enemy were driving mines: it was perfectly successful, and fifteen or twenty of the enemy were killed. Our loss was one Seikh and one 32nd slightly, and one 32nd severely wounded.

This afternoon a very sad event occurred. Major Francis, 13th Native Infantry, who had commanded at the Muchee Bhawun, and who was in command of the brigade mess square, was struck in the legs by a round shot, which completely fractured both legs, rendering amputation of one *immediate,* and great fears were entertained for the other. He was a brave, good officer, and much respected by all, and one in whom Sir Henry Lawrence had much confidence. The calm manner in which he bore his misfortune, gained him the sympathies of all. Not a murmur escaped him; his only anxiety being a hope that the authorities would bear testimony that he had performed his duty. The Rev. Mr. Polehampton, military chaplain, was severely wounded in the side this day, by a rifle ball, while in hospital.

One of the walls of the Racket Court, now used as
a bhoosa gadown, fell in, and a quantity of the bhoosa
became exposed in consequence. All spare tar-
paulings were immediately supplied to cover it, and
officers and men worked hard for two hours, in a
deluge of rain. The rains, so long expected, seem
now fairly set in. It commenced raining heavily at
2 P.M., and continued pouring down the whole
night.

July 8th. — All very much as usual, and very
heavy rain fell, which somewhat abated the enemy's
fire. Every effort was made to put the place
in some kind of order and to feed the bullocks.

Poor Major Francis insensible and sinking: he
died at 7 P.M., and was buried by a party of officers
close to Mr. Ommanney's grave. Every effort was
made to curtail the expenditure of provision, and
officers were placed on half rations every third day.
Very few servants remained, and most of the officers
had none. All were on duty thirteen and twenty
hours a day; and constant alarms took place at night,
rendering it necessary for all to stand to their arms.

Fears were entertained of the bhoosah stack taking fire, as the outer wall of the Racket Court had fallen down and left it exposed. All available officers and men worked hard, in heavy rain, to get it covered in again with tarpaulins. Twelve Seikhs of the 13th Native Infantry deserted last night. All the Hindoos and Mussulmans of the 13th, 48th, and 71st behaved nobly.

July 9th. — Much rain fell during the morning. About 4 A. M. the enemy made an attack on the Baillie Guard Gate, and about 300 showed themselves, shouting and sounding the "Advance," on the bugle; but being received with a few rounds of grape, and a steady fire from the 13th, they speedily disappeared. Very much the same thing occurred soon after at the Cawnpore battery. Continued firing all day.

This was now the tenth day of the siege, and the heavy musketry fire on every side had never for an instant ceased night or day; and at times the fire was terrific. Many casualties occurred, and our want of protection at the different crossings over from one side of the Residency compound to the

other, was very much felt. To-day, an excellent
soldier, and a man greatly respected, Mr. Bryson,
formerly Serjeant-major of the 16th Lancers, was
shot through the head, while endeavouring to
strengthen his post. The enemy appeared to have
had some excellent marksmen. The commissariat
began to work well, and all were well supplied.
The officers were placed, however, on half rations
every third day as a precautionary measure.
Lieutenant Dashwood of the 48th Native Infantry,
died of cholera after a few hours' illness.

July 10*th.* — This morning the enemy's fire was
continued much as usual. A sepoy of the 13th was
killed early in the morning, and later in the day
a private of the 32nd Foot and an artilleryman
were wounded. The horses of the cavalry and the
artillery, which, during the first days of the siege,
were loose and driven nearly mad from hunger and
thirst, galloping about and creating the greatest
confusion, had now been nearly all turned out,
though not without much trouble; and fifty of the
best were retained, and secured in the Seikh

square. All the bullocks were now also secured, and arrangements made for feeding and watering them ; but numbers of horses and bullocks died, and their burial at night by working parties, in addition to nightly fatigue parties for the purpose of burying the dead, carrying up supplies from exposed positions, repairing entrenchments, draining, and altering the position of guns, in addition to attending on the wounded, caused excessive fatigue to the thin garrison, who had but little rest night or day: there were few officers with more than one servant, and one third certainly had *none*. In all duties, the officers equally shared the labours with the men, carrying loads and digging pits for putrid animals, at night, in heavy rain. All exerted themselves to the utmost, alternately exposed to a burning sun and heavy rain. Towards the middle of the day, the enemy fired less than they had previously done on any occasion since the siege commenced.

We received no news from any quarter, but sent off many letters. Every exertion was made to grind up the wheat in store by hand-mills ; and this day thirteen maunds and two seers were ground. The firing towards the afternoon to-day was very slack, comparatively speaking. There was a comparatively slight cannonade. An injured 9-pounder in the Cawnpore battery was removed by us and replaced by another.

July 11*th.* — About 1 o'clock this morning the whole force stood to their arms, in consequence of some information which was received, reporting that an attack was immediately intended. The force remained prepared till daylight, when, as usual, a smart firing on all sides began. An artilleryman was killed at Captain Simmons's battery. The enemy fired several round shot, and were most persevering in keeping us on the alert, and worrying us as much as possible. Their fire had never yet ceased day or night: sometimes it was heavier than at others, but it never abated altogether on any side.

At night the officers buried a horse which had died close to the brigade square; the night was intensely hot and close, and the labour was excessive : — the horse having died on the Pucka road, had to be dragged to a considerable distance

before a grave could be dug. A great many of
the stores were also brought up from the church by
the assistance of a fatigue party of officers, who had
all the carts to load and unload. Two of the 32nd
Foot were killed during the night, which passed off
with a heavy fire.

July 12*th.* — The heat still excessive, and the
fatigue of the garrison was *very* great. Enemy
were most persevering, and loopholed every place
within fifty or sixty yards of our defences. They
were evidently determined to do their best to get into
the position, and had closed in on every side. We
had no intelligence from any quarter; for though we
had sent out many messengers, not one returned.

About 8 o'clock in the evening the enemy made
an attempt to attack the Baillie Gate; but fell back,
on being received with shells and musketry. About
12 P. M. they renewed their efforts on Mr. Gubbins's side with similar effect. They repeatedly
sounded the advance, and were frequently heard
abusing each other for not advancing. In half
an hour they retired, and for the rest of the night

they contented themselves with a heavy fire on the
Cawnpore battery.

July 13*th.* — The heat was dreadful, and garrison
were greatly fatigued.   The enemy reoccupied
Johannes's house, and fired smartly down the street,
killing two sepoys and wounding a conductor:
they also pushed close up under the Redan, and
greatly annoyed our outposts.   Lieutenant Charlton of the 32nd Foot was shot through the head
in the church, and very dangerously wounded.
Several shells were fired into Johannes's house, and
the walls of the house opposite to it were loopholed.
Nevertheless we could not dislodge them, and they
annoyed us greatly.   The Havildar-major of the
13th was wounded through the thigh to-day.

The enemy possessed many excellent marksmen,
and fired so many shots from every point that it was
exceedingly dangerous to be seen anywhere, even
for an instant: they fired several logs of wood
bound with iron, and were evidently at this period
hard up for round shot.   In the evening they fired
several carcases, and succeeded once in setting the

Residency on fire; but it was soon extinguished. All the European officers laboured hard to get the supplies out of the church.

July 14*th*. — Heavy rain, thunder and lightning, and night intensely dark. No alarms, and less firing than usual. Heavy rain at daybreak, which cleared off at 9 o'clock, when the enemy assembled in force. They were apparently undecided how to act, for they moved about in various directions, and in about half an hour retired altogether; but they fired many carcases, shot, and logs of wood shod with iron, and displayed several new batteries. We threw up a traverse near the Post-office gate, in order to save our people from the fire from Johannes's house, which was very sharp. Our sharp-shooters killed four of the enemy in Johannes's house. Four Seikhs of the 13th deserted, leaving their arms and accoutrements. Still no information of any kind.

Enemy erecting new batteries; one of which opened about 5 P. M. with a 9-pounder on the gable end of the brigade mess, occupied by the ladies and children, and the roof of which was held by a party

of officers, assisted by six men of the 32nd. At the
first discharge, a soldier of the 32nd had his thigh
fractured, rendering amputation necessary. They
fired several iron shot, which tore away the parapet;
but fortunately no one else was hurt. The night
was very dark, and the enemy fired a great deal;
more particularly on Mr. Gubbins's post, where
Lieutenant Lester was mortally wounded: towards daylight the fire abated. Several cases of
cholera. The enemy's fire to-day destroyed a
9-pounder of ours, smashing the axle tree all to
pieces.

July 15*th.* — The enemy opened fire from their
9-pounder battery, situated about fifty yards from
the end of the brigade mess, and fired many shots;
but the garrison laid close, and up to 3 P.M. no
casualties occurred. Towards the middle of the
day, the enemy's fire lulled to a greater extent than
it had ever done since the siege commenced.

The stores out of Anderson's house got in; the
house being entirely destroyed by round shot;
though still nobly held by the garrison. A mortar

moved down to the gate of the Post-office, behind
the traverse, and several shells were thrown into
Johannes's house.   All much as usual.   The enemy
fired three rounds of grape into the Redan battery
during the night, but fortunately hit no one.

July 16*th.* — The heat during the night was
fearful.   A slight alarm about 2 A.M., but it was
soon over.   The enemy fired smartly throughout
the night, and in the morning sent several round
shot through the roof of the brigade mess, and hit
the Residency.   They were busy, besides, making
batteries in the garden of Johannes's house, and
opposite the 13th and the Cawnpore battery.

We shelled the enemy heavily during the forenoon,
throwing them far into the town and across the
river.   Lieutenant Bryce was badly wounded in the
thigh early this morning; and later in the day,
Lieutenant O'Brien of the 84th was shot through
the arm.   In the evening the enemy kept up a
heavy fusilade, and we shelled them smartly; they
fired a shell which narrowly escaped falling into our
bhoosah stack.   At half-past 11 o'clock, they fired a

good deal on the Cawnpore battery, and made a feint
of attacking, but finding us well on the alert did not
do so.   Our wheat-grinding operations continued,
and we now had hand-mills sufficiently well
worked to grind twenty maunds of atta daily.
During the night we threw up a stockade and traverse, as a protection against the musketry which
swept the entrance of the Residency.

July 17th.— The heat excessive.   A very heavy
fire during the night, and the garrison kept on the
alert, preventing rest and greatly fatiguing all.
Several cases of cholera and deaths of children occurred.   Twenty-two maunds of wheat were ground.
   To-day a bad accident occurred : Lieutenant Alexander, of the Artillery, and Captain Barlow, 50th
Native Infantry, in firing a mortar, were most severely burnt by the piece going off at the time of
loading.   The enemy sent two shells into the Residency which exploded, but fortunately caused no
loss of life.   The stench from putrid animals was
most offensive.   Painful boils about the head were
very prevalent.   The wounded doing well.   The

prisoners and main guard removed to another place, in order to give more room at the hospital.

The enemy were busy making more batteries and intrenchments. In the night about 12 o'clock, the enemy made an attack on Mr. Gubbins's position, but were received with a steady fire, and soon driven back.

July 18*th.*—Rain began falling about 4 A.M. and continued to do so till 8 A.M., when the heat became insufferable. The enemy fired several round shot, which hit the brigade mess; and they also took up an annoying position in one of the towers which remained of the Ferad Buksh gate. They were, however, speedily dislodged by a few exceedingly well-directed shots from Lieutenant Bonham, from an 18-pounder in the Post-office. Two children died of cholera. In the evening the enemy fired many round shot into the Post-office, Dr. Fayrer's, Mr. Gubbins's and the brigade mess house: they evidently had been reinforced in guns. At night, Brigadier Inglis, Captain Wilson, Lieutenant Innes, and Ensign Birch, proceeded to the gate with eight

Europeans, and dragged in a body that was seen lying near the gate, and which it was supposed might be the body of one of our spies shot coming in. It was safely brought in, and found to be the corpse of a woman. Nothing was found on the body. The enemy got into the turret on the top of Mr. Johannes' house, and fired into the Cawnpore battery : fortunately no casualties occurred, and the night, which was fearfully oppressive, passed away with a heavy fire from the enemy.

July 19*th*.—Dreadful heat: cloudy, but no rain. Enemy fired round shot all the morning. About half-past 9 a large shot passed through a room in the Residency, in which the officers were at breakfast, fracturing the leg of Lieutenant Harmer, 32nd Foot, but providentially injuring no one else ; about the same time Lieutenant Arthur, 7th Cavalry, was shot dead (through the heart) in the Cawnpore battery. Our 18-pounder fired several shots, and we threw several shells. The enemy seemed to be at work at the Muchee Bhawun, probably looking for shot which had been buried in the ruins.

D

About 12 o'clock to-day the enemy sounded the
advance, and threatened an attack on the Redan.
A few shells, however, soon made them give up all
idea of coming on. They got into Johannes' house
in force, and fired steadily into the cook-house of
the brigade mess.

Much drunkenness prevailed amongst a few of
the garrison, who had stolen quantities of liquor,
which could not be discovered. From the commencement of the siege, the large quantities of
liquor in the hands of the merchants caused much
anxiety, and every possible endeavour was made to
get it all into safe custody. One or two alarms
during the early part of the night. Mr. Polehampton
(wounded and in hospital) died this day from cholera.

July 20*th.*—From midnight the enemy remained
unusually quiet, and at daylight all seemed much as
usual. About half-past 8 A.M. it was reported that a very
large body of men could be seen marching about in
different directions within a few hundred yards of our
position. A sharp look-out was kept, and the garrison stood to their arms. At a quarter-past 10, the
enemy sprung a mine inside the water gate, and about

twenty-five yards from our inner defences: the explosion was great, and was evidently intended to have blown up our Redan battery, and also to act as a signal; for immediately the dust and smoke subsided, a very heavy fire of round shot was commenced from every gun that the enemy possessed, followed immediately almost by a terrific fire of musketry, under which the enemy made an attempt to storm the Redan and Innes' house. The garrison were ready, and every one at his post, and the attack was coolly met and repulsed; however the enemy advanced boldly and came up within twenty-five yards of the battery in immense force, but were unable to withstand the fire of our men.

They made a similar attempt on Innes' house, but were similarly repulsed by the garrison, consisting of twelve men of the 32nd, twelve of the 13th Native Infantry, and a few uncovenanted gentlemen, under Ensign Loughnan (who distinguished himself greatly): very great loss was inflicted on the enemy, who repeatedly tried to advance, but were driven back each time with much slaughter. Finding their efforts useless, the enemy fell back,

and contented themselves with throwing in a terrific storm of musketry; from which we shielded
our men as much as possible, by keeping them laid
under our defences. Almost at the same time an
attack was made on the Cawnpore Battery, but the
enemy's standard-bearer (who advanced bravely)
being shot in the ditch of the battery, the rest fell
back. The enemy now moved towards Lieutenant
Anderson's house and Captain Germon's post, with
scaling-ladders, but were well received and fell back
with much loss. The attack was now over, though
for the rest of the day, until 4 P. M., the enemy threw
in a heavy fire; when it gradually subsided: the
attack was mostly confined to the points above noted.

In the afternoon they succeeded in making a lodgment in some pucka cook-houses inside our abattis,
and began to use a crowbar, which was distinctly
heard. We made a hole through to them from above,
through which they fired, injuring no one; but on
our throwing down some hand grenades, they fled
across the road, two being shot by the officers who
were watching from above. The 13th, 71st, and
48th sepoys all behaved well, and the manner in
which the outposts were held, was beyond all praise.

The uncovenanted distinguished themselves greatly. We had fortunately only four men killed, and some twelve wounded: Captain Forbes, Lieutenant Grant, Lieutenant Edmonstone, and Mr. Hely, were wounded. All were under arms from eight in the morning until eight at night, and greatly fatigued and worn out.

July 21*st.*—All very quiet during the night. The enemy were probably fatigued with their exertions yesterday, for throughout the night only a few round shot were thrown in. About 10 A.M. the enemy lodged themselves in some force in the low buildings between the Seikh courtyard and Mr. Gubbins's post, but were driven out by a few shells, and were fired on by the officers of the brigade mess, as they ran across a small lane: they did not attempt to reoccupy the position during the day. About 12 o'clock, Major Banks was killed by a musket-shot through the head, as he was reconnoitring from the top of an outhouse. Mr. Gubbins's garrison was fired on smartly during the morning, and many round shot were sent into Mr. Gubbins's house;

the garrison of which had many alarms during the day. Painful boils very prevalent. A dreadful stench pervaded the place in consequence of the number of dead horses and bullocks, which, lying direct under the fire of the enemy, we were unable to remove. Excessive heat, and several cases of cholera. Great fatigue; no news. Poor Dr. Brydon severely wounded in Mr. Gubbins's house. Two Europeans killed, and two wounded; also one of the 13th sepoys.

July 22*nd.*—Very heavy rain began to fall at 1 A.M., and continued till 8 A.M., when it cleared off. During the heavy rain, the enemy only fired slightly. After 8 A.M. it became more brisk, and they fired several round shot, but were not very active during the forenoon. Cholera still prevalent. Our numerical strength much diminished, as we had had 151 casualties in the 32nd Regiment alone. The enemy moved the 8-inch howitzer from its old position, and brought it across the river by elephants, with a tumbril behind it. Up to this date, we had no intelligence of any kind from any quarter, and, indeed, we had received none since the 27th ultimo.

Many messengers were sent with letters, but not a single line did we receive in reply. A letter was sent off to Cawnpore to-day, and conveyed by a man named Ram Singh, a Seikh subadar of the 63rd Native Infantry. The enemy steadily loop-holing all the houses close round about, and evidently up to some new attempt at our position.

At dusk heavy rain; we got out a strong working party, and opened our large powder magazine, and after much labour and exertion got up 150 barrels out of the 240 we had buried. The night was pitch dark, and the rain fell heavily, and the work being outside of our entrenchment, over which all the barrels had to be handed out of mud knee deep, rendered the work fearfully fatiguing. Many of the officers and civilians worked for five hours at this work. Only a few shots during the night. Boils still very prevalent. A Seikh from the cavalry deserted. One or two cases of cholera. Mortification having set in, Mr. Hely's arm was amputated.

The buildings outside Mr. Gubbins's position were shelled at sunset, and after we had driven the enemy out, we made a sortie through the wall (in which we

had cut a large hole), and rushed out and examined
the houses in which the enemy had been. We
failed to find any trace of mining. We lost one
man of the 32nd, killed. Mrs. Dorin was killed
dead by a musket ball in Mr. Gubbins's house to-day.

July 23rd.—Very heavy rain during the night.
About 2 A. M. the enemy sounded the "turn out,"
and at 3 the "assembly." About 1 A. M. a native
pensioner, who left us on the 27th to gain information, came in, and said he had been confined by the
enemy thirteen days, but had been to Cawnpore and
left it two days ago,—that a British force with twelve
guns was there; that they had fought three times
with the Nana's troops, and had completely beaten
them, taking many guns, and that they were crossing the river preparatory to advancing to our assistance. He stated that he had not brought a
letter, for fear of being detained by the enemy; he
vouched to the truth of his statement, declined a
pecuniary reward, and was urgent to go back
quickly while it rained heavily and all was quiet
comparatively. He left in two hours, taking a
small note for the officer commanding the forces.

At daylight there were fewer of the enemy than we had yet seen about, and those less active; though they still fired smartly all around. Stench from dead animals in some parts dreadful; as we had very few servants of any kind and our fighting men were so few and so harassed, that we were helpless to bury them. Heavy showers both day and night, keeping the garrison constantly drenched to the skin, and making all most uncomfortable; particularly as few had a change of clothes. Enemy fired slackly during the afternoon. Cannonaded their bridge of boats, which was broken by our 18-pounder shot. Several cases of small-pox. Sick and wounded much crowded. The upper story of the hospital being under fire of round shot, the wounded were, from the commencement of the siege, confined to the ground floor, which with difficulty contained their beds. At night it rained hard; and in spite of all difficulties, we succeeded in getting up the remaining ninety barrels of powder, and safely deposited them in the centre of our position. A false alarm about 12 o'clock at night, that the enemy had got into the churchyard.

July 24th.—Morning fair and cloudy. The enemy endeavoured to repair the bridge of boats, but were prevented by the fire of our 18-pounder. The heat and stench terrible, and the flies were beyond endurance, contesting every particle of food with us, and preventing all attempts at rest during the day. Only a few round shot thrown, but the enemy actively at work about forty yards from the Redan battery, in a deep trench. Advantage taken of the temporary lull to repair some of our defences, which had sunk a great deal in consequence of the heavy rain; but our men, reduced in numbers and harassed to death day and night, were not capable of any prolonged exertion. Every possible effort was made to grind wheat, and from twenty-five to thirty hand-mills were kept steadily at work, producing an average of twenty maunds of flour daily. The 48th Regiment Native Infantry have had seven, and the 71st Regiment, upwards of fifty desertions, since the commencement of the siege.

About dusk, the enemy, for the first time, sent in many shells; which, however, caused no loss, fortunately. The commissariat department busy with

the stores, getting ghee up from the Round House;
while a fatigue party of officers, under Captain
Radcliffe, threw up earth, and heightened the
traverse across the road, near the Post-office gate.
Lieutenant Hutchinson, of the Engineers, accompanied by Lieutenant Birch, crept down in the dark,
and examined, as well as they could, the enemy's
works in the immediate vicinity of the Redan.
Night dark and cloudy.

July 25th. — The night passed away tolerably
quietly; the enemy firing several 18-pound shot
into the Cawnpore battery. At daylight they were
tolerably quiet, contenting themselves with musketry;
but about 8 A.M. they fired an 8-inch shell, which fell
through the centre of the roof of the Post-office, and
lodged on the table on which the officers of that post
breakfasted; fortunately it did not explode, and no
mischief was done. Immediately after, several shells,
apparently thrown out of mortars, were thrown in,
and continued to be so during the forenoon. One
fell in the verandah of the Post-office, and shattered
the hand of an artilleryman. Two men of the

32nd were shot this morning by the enemy's sharp-
shooters. Still not one word of intelligence from
any quarter, though this was now the twenty-sixth
day we had been besieged. We knew nothing ; but
the most absurd rumours were afloat amongst the
natives, and indeed among many of the Europeans,
who were credulous enough to believe them. Removed the powder out of the place in which we had
it, to a tykhana under the Begum Kotee which the
engineers considered safer than where it was first
removed to. Very slight firing on the river side,
but the enemy still very active near the Redan.
Much difference of opinion existed as to the object
of the work ; the majority believed that they were
mining, while the engineers thought they were only
making a trench. Although the earlier part of the
morning had been quiet enough, towards 11 and 12
o'clock, a very sharp fire was opened and maintained
on the side of the Post-office and Cawnpore battery.

The casualties on this side alone amounted to
six, besides three others in different places, which
made the total of the day's casualties one of the
heaviest on record. Towards evening the enemy

commenced shelling us. Seven shells were sent in, but did no damage. Opinions differed whether they were discharged from howitzers or mortars.

About 11 P.M. a pensioner, who had been sent out from this on the 22nd instant with a letter, effected his entrance into Mr. Gubbins's compound, and produced a letter which he had brought back from the camp. He was at once brought to Brigadier Inglis and examined. The letter proved to be one from Lieutenant-Colonel Fraser Tytler, Quartermaster-General with General Havelock's force. It was determined to transmit to General Havelock by this man a plan of our position and of the roads approaching it, with memoranda drawn up by the engineers.

July 26th. — At daybreak cloudy and sultry: enemy tolerably quiet, but about 8 A.M. they threw in several shells. From 11 to 1 very heavy rain, and a partial cessation from firing, during which Lieutenant Lewin of the Artillery, who was reconnoitring from the Cawnpore battery, was shot dead by one of the enemy's sharp-shooters. Enemy recommenced shelling from the city side : few of them to be seen, all being under cover.   Supposed to be mining at the Cawnpore battery.   A countermine commenced by us, out of the house next the battery ; but having no workmen except our harassed soldiers, the work was slow ; however, as the engineers seemed to entertain little or no doubt but that the enemy were mining, it was necessary to endeavour to counteract them.   Little musketry fire during the afternoon ; the enemy throwing in heavy shot, fired at a great elevation (apparently out of howitzer).   One or two cases of cholera. Garrison in good spirits at the prospect of early relief.

A letter and plan of our position forwarded at night by a messenger to the officer commanding the relieving force : 5000 rupees promised the messenger if he brought a reply.   Suddenly at 10 P.M. the enemy commenced a heavy fire along the whole of the city front of our position ; but nothing came of it, as after a few shells had been thrown amongst them, their fire gradually subsided, and all became tolerably quiet again.   During this heavy firing, a sad accident occurred ; Lieutenant Shepherd of the 7th Cavalry being shot dead in the brigade square, by a shot fired

from the top of the brigade mess by one of our
garrison. This was the only casualty of the night.

July 27th. — From midnight all quiet, save the
usual musketry fire. Cloudy, sultry weather. About
7 A.M. two planks were observed laid across the road
in front of Johannes' house. They were not seen the
night before, and being carefully watched, a man's
hand was seen coming up from below; and soon after
some eight feet of earth fell in, showing the direction
of a mine of the enemy right across the road, and
pointing direct for our stockade, within six feet of
which it had apparently reached. This was a most
fortunate discovery for us: they had evidently kept
this mine too near the surface, and the heavy rain had
broke it in. Our mine continued to be pushed on as
rapidly as possible, and our sharp-shooters from the
top of the brigade mess kept up so hot a fire on the
enemy's sap from above, that they could make no attempt to repair the mischief. Much fever prevalent,
consequent on being constantly wet day and night.

Towards the afternoon, the enemy again covered
their trench with boards; but we got a mortar

under our wall, and after one or two failures, a shell
fell right into the hole and blew all the planks away,
leaving the remains of the trench exposed to view,
giving us no further anxiety. Fine weather in the
afternoon. Enemy heard mining towards the brigadier
mess; on which a shaft was commenced by the officers,
and the enemy ceased working. Late in the evening,
the enemy were very distinctly heard mining towards
the Seikh lines; on which the Seikhs, under Lieutenant Hardinge, commenced and sunk an eight feet
shaft; hearing us, the enemy seemed to stop working. All quiet, with the exception of the usual
amount of firing. Fever, diarrhœa, dysentery, and
painful boils, from constant wet and exposure, still
prevalent amongst the garrison. Mrs. Grant (wife
of Lieutenant Grant) died of cholera. Captain
Boileau, 7th Cavalry, was wounded to-day.

July 28th. — Much shouting and bugling amongst
the enemy during the early part of the morning:
heavy rain at daylight. Made repairs to the Redan
battery, also made a small field work for a 9-
pounder. Sickness much increased, and for many

days past only one engineer officer was available for
duty : hard work, privation, and exposure day and
night to wet and heat, few could long stand against.
We had no further news of our coming friends, but
trusted that to-day they would reach Bunnee.

The enemy threw in several shells, also a number
of stink-pots, which were a very curious composition
of large pieces of our exploded iron shell sewn up in
canvas, and surrounded by flax and resin, with dry
powder in the centre : these, from the commencement
of the siege, had been thrown in daily from a howitzer ; they made a fearful hissing noise and great
stench, and finally exploded. They were not very
dangerous, unless they exploded *very* close to a
person. We also had a few rockets thrown in, but
not many ; and lately a number of shrapnel shells,
fired apparently from a howitzer with a very great
elevation. The enemy's miners could now be distinctly heard working close to the Seikh Square sap.

The room in the Residency containing the jewellery
and valuables belonging to the late King of Oude, was
broken into last night by some of the garrison, and
most of them stolen. Enemy tolerably quiet in the

afternoon. About 5 P.M. our sap in the Seikh Square, which had been going on as fast as we could push it in the direction of the enemy's, met theirs, which they continued to work to the last moment. On our crow-bar, however, going through into their gallery, they instantly fled out of it, and commenced to fill in their shaft. We immediately made use of their gallery, and blew the whole up with 100 lbs. of powder, which brought down all the adjacent houses, &c. After this the enemy tolerably quiet. Good progress made in our Cawnpore sap.

July 29th. — A fine moonlight night. Enemy fired many round shot about daylight, and also musketry from the houses across the road; they also threw in many carcases, which nearly all fell in the vicinity of the Cawnpore battery. No intelli-gence. All were anxious for the relieving force, which we thought could not be far off. Our Cawnpore sap loaded with 200lbs. of powder, ready to explode whenever it might be thought most advisable. Colonel Halford, 71st Regiment Native Infantry, who had been long ill, died this morning.

A few convalescents joined the ranks, giving more

room in the hospital, which was greatly overcrowded
in consequence of all the patients being obliged to
be kept on the ground floor, as also the state
prisoners and their servants; the round shot passing
so frequently through the upper story as to make
it impossible to make use of it. Rumour stated
that the enemy had gone out in force to meet our
coming army, and had left two or three regiments
of infantry, and a body of military police, to keep
us in; but it was most difficult to tell what force
we had opposed to us, as the enemy seldom or never
showed in any number, but kept in the houses under
cover, occasionally yelling, bugling, and throwing in
a heavy fire, then subsiding into the usual steady
fire which went on night and day.

Firing of cannon heard in the direction of Cawnpore. We hoped it was our friends. All anxious, but
all conjecture. Enemy recommenced mining towards
our mine in the Cawnpore battery. About 6 P. M.,
a heavy firing was heard for about five minutes in
the road from Cawnpore, and in about half an hour,
several guns were heard in the direction of cantonments; this made us think it was a salute fired by

the enemy for some reason or other; probably
to reassure themselves.   However, all is conjecture; but it threw our garrison into a great state of
excitement, and many (indeed most) stoutly maintained it was our force.   About 300 or 400 sepoys
were seen at the same time running across the
iron bridge towards cantonments in great haste.
We fired two shots at them with an 18-pounder.

The excitement gradually cooled down; the enemy
keeping up their usual fire.   Another mine was
discovered this evening, by a portion of it falling in:
it was running in the direction of Sago's house.
Lieutenant Grant of the Bombay army, whose wife
and child died a few days ago of cholera, died in
hospital this night, from the effects of his wound:
his right hand had been blown off by a hand-
grenade.   A fine moonlight night.

July 30*th*. — From 2 A. M. till daylight heavy
rain.   Enemy got in close under the wall of the
Seikh lines, and began some kind of operations
against it; they were so close that no musket
could be fired, being under a projecting piece of the

wall; they were, however, dislodged by a few
pistol shots, and ran off. No further incident occurred during the night, beyond that there was the
usual amount of firing into our position, and bugling
on the part of the enemy. After daylight enemy
fired slackly. Terrible stench in many parts of
the garrison from half-buried corpses and animals,
which we had no time or means to bury properly.
Several cases of fever, cholera, and smallpox.

About 9 A. M. a number of sepoys and matchlockmen were seen coming along the Cawnpore road,
and for about an hour and a half a continuous stream
of men came in in detached parties of twenty and
thirty : some sepoys were among them. Slack
firing during the forenoon, only a few shells and
musketry. In the afternoon, heavy rain for an
hour. Unable to discover what the enemy were
about. Considerable progress made in a sap, which
we had sunk in an outhouse close to the corner of
the brigade mess-house, where most of the children
and ladies were located. At first the enemy were
heard mining towards us, but since yesterday we
had not heard them. We continued, however, to

steadily push our sap, hoping either to come across
that of the enemy or succeed in getting under
Johannes' house; from which they fired all day long
on any one who showed himself. Yesterday an
artillery sergeant, who incautiously crossed the
road commanded from Johannes' house, was shot
through both legs. The enemy had many riflemen,
and some of them were most expert shots, firing
through our loopholes.

About 8 P. M., as Captain Wilson, Lieutenant
Barwell, Lieutenant James, and Mr. Lawrence were
sitting on the chubootra of the Begum Kotee, a shell
came in and exploded as it struck the parapet of
the wall under which they sat, bringing it down.
Lieutenant James, who was lying wounded on his
bed, had a most wonderful escape. A large piece
of masonry, weighing upwards of a hundred weight,
fell on his bed, breaking it to pieces, and bringing
him down on the ground; but he was uninjured.
Mr. Lawrence received a severe contusion on the
back and head from falling masonry; and this was
the extent of the damage.   Mrs. Clarke, wife of
Lieutenant Clarke of the 21st Native Infantry,

died this evening: bad food, privation, confinement, and smells of all kinds, worked their effects.

July 31*st.* —A fine night, and the usual firing. At daylight, the enemy commenced firing heavily on the Church and Residency, from a 24-pounder planted in the neighbourhood of the iron bridge. They also threw in many shells, and fired their guns from the Clock Tower Gate. Our 18-pounders and mortars were employed until 10 A.M. in silencing the enemy's fire. Our sap from the brigade mess made good progress across the road, towards the outhouses occupied by the enemy. Several children have lately died : privation the chief cause. We had received no information whatever since the 26th instant, the date on which we received the only letter we had yet received since the 27th of June. Our re-inforcements were due to-day, and their non-arrival led us to suppose that the enemy had succeeded in breaking down the bridge at Bunnee, and arresting the progress of our friends. The flies dreadful, — preventing all rest during the day, and disputing our food with us. The enemy continued to throw in shells all the forenoon, till 2 P.M. when we had a heavy shower: after that, the firing continued as before. In the evening we repaired our defences as far as we could, as, owing to the heavy rain, the earth had settled very considerably. A fine moonlight night, and all quiet, save the usual amount of round shot and musketry.

August 1st.—Still no intelligence of any kind, which caused much anxiety, more particularly as some of our supplies for natives were likely to be at an end in twenty days' time. Weather very hot and sultry; small painful boils, covering nearly the whole body, very prevalent. Many deaths among the children, and sickness on the increase. Great inconvenience felt in the hospital for want of space; the sick and wounded sadly crowded, and the building very badly ventilated, as the lower story was hardly safe from shots. Enemy threw in many shells this morning, and fired unusually sharp with their heavy guns, till about 10 A.M., keeping our guns and mortars fully employed in keeping down their fire. Heat very great; fire gradually slack-

ened off towards noon, but recommenced sharply
again about 5 P.M.   Many round shot, shell, and
carcases came in.   One of the latter fell into the
court-yard of the Begum Kotee, within a few feet
of the table at which the staff and commissariat officers were at dinner; but no one was hurt.   Several
cases of cholera occurred to-day.   Efforts made to im-
prove and strengthen our defences during the moonlight nights; but the engineer officers were all sick,
and little was done.   Our sap in the brigade mess was
pushed steadily on, and had attained thirty-eight
feet from the shaft this evening.

August 2nd. — Fine moonlight night.   Sharp
firing during some portion of it.   Many rockets
were thrown in early in the morning.   Mr. Hely of
the 7th Cavalry died this day of the wound he
received on the 20th ult.   An artillery sergeant was
mortally wounded this morning in the Redan.
Enemy fired a salute of some forty guns
about 11 A.M.   A Seikh sowar of the 3rd Irregular
Cavalry deserted to the enemy this morning.   The
Bhoosa stack fell down to-day, burying ten or

twelve bullocks; which, after much labour, were
got out.   Seven of them were unfortunately dead;
thus entailing more labour, as at night we had to
bury them: no slight task in such weather, with
our jaded and harassed garrison.   Towards the
evening a heavy cannonade was kept up on both
sides.   About 5·30 P.M. an eight-inch shell from
the enemy struck the Begum Kotee, and, breaking
right through the outside wall, exploded in the
room in which Lieutenant James of the Commissariat and Mr. Lawrence of the Civil Service were
lying on their beds wounded, with one or two servants in the room; providentially all escaped, though
the room was set on fire.   Heavy firing till midnight.

August 3rd.—Smart firing till daylight.   Every
possible effort was made to strengthen our position
and raise the height of our defences.   A soldier of
the 32nd Foot was shot dead this morning in the
centre room of the hospital; showing how little
safety anywhere existed against the enemy's fire.

A new loop-hole on the top of the brigade mess,
which it was discovered commanded a distant and

much frequented lane in the city, was made use of by Lieutenant Sewell, armed with his Enfield rifle; the distance being not above 750 yards, the conical bullets most effectually cleared the lanes of the sepoys, as they lounged up it, and quickened the paces of the citizens as they crossed and recrossed.

Enemy unusually slack in firing after dark till about 10 P.M., when they recommenced firing, and continued it during the night. The engineers continued their endeavours to strengthen our position, by heightening the abattis near the Redan. A fine moonlight night. Several cannon shots were heard in the distance, but no intelligence of any kind reached us.

August 4th. — The enemy fired a great number of rounds from their guns at intervals during the night. Musketry fire was slack this morning. No news of any kind. Could get no messengers to go out with a letter, though it was made so small that it went into half a quill; but it had been spread abroad that the enemy would kill any one leaving the garrison, and this deterred any one from endea-

vouring to carry a letter to our friends, no matter
how great the reward might be that was held out.

Many officers and men are laid up with fever and
dysentery.   Our stored attah was nearly expended,
and in a few days' time we should have to commence
that which we had ground, which now amounted to
about 500 maunds.   At 2 P.M. the firing of all
kinds was very slack; indeed, for long intervals, not
a shot was to be heard.   The officers, also, who
relieve one another as look-outs on the top of the
Residency, reported that a smaller number of men
than usual were to be seen on the move.   An
Eurasian, attached to the party working Dr.
Fayrer's guns, was shot dead while working the
18-pounder guns this day, by a man said to be
not sixty yards off.   Several convalescents have
been moved from the hospital to other quarters, and
with happy results both as regards themselves and
those left in the hospital, which greatly wanted a
free circulation of air.   Towards dusk many shells
came in, and one exploded in the second brigade
square; fortunately, it was seen coming, and no
harm ensued.   The powder magazine was made as

secure as possible, by putting heavy beams across
the roof, and covering them with two feet of
earth.   A fine night, but very much firing till midnight.

August 5th.—Sent off another letter to the officer
commanding the relieving force, of which we could
gain no intelligence; though we conjecture the advance of our force had been arrested by the enemy
at the bridge of Bunnee.   Heavy showers during
the day.   Musket-proof shutters were completed
for the embrasure of the 18-pounders to the left of
the hospital.   Many of the convalescent patients removed to the Thug Gaol Barracks, which gave them
a slight change, and created more room in the hospital.   Efforts made to clear some of the drains, and
reduce the stench which pervades the garrison.   At
sunset the enemy were seen at a distance in some
force, with drums and fifes playing, marching from
the direction of the river towards the Cawnpore
road.   Soon after, they threw many shells into us,
and continued to do so for some time.   About 8 P.M.
all became tolerably quiet.

August 6th.—The enemy fired several shots, from
a 24-pounder, at the Residency, one of which unfortunately fractured the arm of Ensign Studdy of
the 32nd Foot, as he sat down to breakfast; rendering amputation necessary. This gun caused us
great annoyance, from its calibre, and firing so frequently as it did into the Residency. Unfortunately
its distance from our position, and its situation in
the midst of buildings, rendered it impossible to
take it by the bayonet; neither could our gunners
see it, so that to shell it was our only resource.

Less firing than usual. The enemy again ascended
into the upper story of Johannes' house, and from
thence caused much annoyance to the position of the
brigade mess, where the cooking went on. They succeeded in killing a sweeper. Terrible heat; Brigadier Inglis suffered from its effects. Various rumours
afloat in the garrison; some of which seemed to have
originated either with a servant of Mr. Gubbins, or
some member of his post. The Residency is at last
to be entirely vacated by the officers of the 32nd
and others now resident there. Last night was
spent in earthing in the magazine, as several shots

had lately gone unpleasantly near. A carcase came into the Begum Kotee in the afternoon, into the room in which Lieutenant James (wounded), Mr. Lawrence (wounded), and Ensign Keir (sick), were lying; it set some of the things in the room on fire, but was speedily extinguished without injury to any one. Much bugling, drumming, and firing towards evening. After dark the enemy fired heavily from their guns in front of the Residency. Our engineers and a working party were busy all this night at Innes' house, making a battery for an 18-pounder, to be moved down in order to endeavour to silence a 24-pounder of the enemy's, which had been doing much mischief by firing through the church and Residency. About 9 P. M. a sepoy of the 1st Oude Irregular Infantry, who took out a letter to the officer commanding the relieving force, came in; he stated that he had delivered it, and that he had received a letter in reply which he had lost in coming in to us. Half-an-hour later, another man, a sepoy of the 48th, who had been sent into the town two days previously to try and gain intelligence, returned, and stated he had been confined

several days by the enemy; and he in a great
measure corroborated the statement of the sepoy of
the 1st Oude Irregular Infantry: this loss of the
letter was a great mortification to us, as it might
have explained what was at this time inexplicable—
the retirement towards Cawnpore of General Havelock's force, after apparently the greatest success on
this side the Ganges.

August 7th.—We worked hard at our new battery
at Innes' house, and got it ready; an 18-pounder
was taken down and in position by daylight, whence
it commenced firing, and soon silenced the enemy's
guns. The enemy, however, fired heavily from some
others, and about 8 A.M. a shell burst close to the
Residency and mortally wounded two of the best
men in the 32nd, the one a colour-sergeant and the
other an orderly-room clerk. Captain Waterman
of the 13th was wounded through the hand by a
musket ball at Innes' post this morning. Several
cases of cholera. Every effort made to increase the
number of men to grind wheat for the force. Exceedingly heavy rain during the middle of the day.

The hose into our mine near Johannes's house got damped, and required all the tamping to be removed. Our position greatly flooded, which rendered it most wretched for those who had to be in trenches night and day. The artillery canteen closed, in consequence of the gross irregularities which prevailed, and its contents removed to the canteen of the 32nd Regiment, from which the artillery were in future supplied. The heavy rain seemed to make the stench which pervaded the place worse, and this evening it was fearful. Several cases of cholera occurred to-day. The enemy's cannon knocked down a portion of the verandah of the Residency, also the verandah of Delprat's house at the Cawnpore battery : a few shells came in in the evening.

August 8th. — A tolerably quiet night. Dr. McDonnell, of the 41st Native Infantry, died early this morning of cholera. A soldier of the 32nd was shot, and a native woman-servant of Mrs. Banks had her thigh broken by musketry at Mr. Gubbins's post this forenoon.

A heavy smoke was distinctly seen in the far

distance in the direction of the Cawnpore road.
Many reports were made of heavy firing being
heard in the same direction : a Sikh attached to
the cavalry brought repeated accounts of it, but no
European, save Captains Forbes and Hawes, of Mr.
Gubbins's post, could say he heard it. The natives
(some of them) very anxious about the arrival of the
reinforcements, of whom we could hear nothing.

In the afternoon, a regiment of infantry, about
600 strong, with drums beating, marching in
quarter distance column with colours, was seen
marching through the city, in the direction of the
Cawnpore road.

Seven hundred yards from the brigade-mess was
a street in the city which was commanded by
Lieutenant Sewell's double Enfield rifle, and on
which spot he had killed several sepoys and others :
this was this afternoon barricaded right across, which
was a nuisance, as it entirely obstructed our view of
what passed along. Lieutenant Bryce of the artillery, who had been severely wounded, died of cholera.

No intelligence came in this evening, and much
anxiety as to our reinforcements was evinced by

some of our native troops and servants. Rice
was served out to most of the natives in lieu of
flour, and wheat to the native camp-followers, in
order to husband our stock of flour. All the tea
and coffee for the Europeans expended ; the last
issue being made yesterday. This was the first day
on which we had no casualty.

August 9th. — The heat excessive, and children
sunk rapidly under the effects of want of good air,
food and exercise : several deaths occurred among
them, both yesterday and to-day. The enemy fired
heavily in the morning, but providentially no one
was hurt. Ensign Studdy, who had had his arm
amputated from the effects of a 24-pounder shot,
died this morning. The enemy were thought to
have recommenced mining near the Redan battery.

Divine service was performed in the brigade mess-
house to all officers not on duty. No signs or
symptoms of our reinforcements. In the middle of
the day Ensign Loughnan of the 13th (on duty at
Innes's house) went out with a few men and quietly
spiked a small gun of the enemy's, and returned

without any loss. A very heavy shower in the
evening, which filled our trenches. One or two
doolies were seen going across the Goomtee, accompanied by sepoys.   About 9 P.M. a Seikh sowar
of the 3rd Oude Irregular Cavalry came in by the
Seikh battery. His having been permitted to pass
the enemy's outposts induced a belief that he had
come in to try and make the other Seikhs desert;
consequently he was placed under British bayonets,
and not allowed to converse with any one.

August 10*th.*—About 10 A.M. a great number of
sepoys, probably 1600, were seen, with two guns,
marching up our left flank and across the Cawnpore
road, behind their trenches. Very shortly after, a large
force was seen to be approaching the bridge of boats
from cantonments; and, in consequence, all were
quickly at their posts. About half an hour after,
the enemy fired a shell into the Begum Kotee,
which appeared to be a signal; for the instant after,
a mine was sprung opposite to Johannes's house,
which blew in a great portion of the house occupied
by Mr. Schilling and the Martinere boys, and entirely destroyed our pallisades and defences for the

space of sixty feet. One of the heaviest timbers was pitched right on the top of the brigade mess-house, among the officers and men of the 32nd, who occupied the post. As soon as the smoke blew away, the enemy pushed up, under a tremendous musketry fire, right into Johannes's house and garden, and into all the buildings close round the Cawnpore battery; but all their efforts to enter our position were met with such a steady fire, that they fell back, and kept up an incessant fire of musketry on our defences. About thirty of them, however, lodged themselves in the ditch of the Cawnpore battery, within a few feet of our guns. A hand grenade was rolled over right into the centre of them, on which they bolted and ran back, exposed to a sharp fusillade from our people on the top of the brigade-mess.

While this was going on, a very sharp attack was made on Mrs. Sago's house, where the enemy blew up a mine, which destroyed some of the outhouses and blew two soldiers out into the road, outside our defences : extraordinary to re-late, they fell unhurt, and got safely back to their

posts. The enemy then made their attack, but
were soon driven back with considerable loss, and
confined themselves to keeping up a tremendous
storm of round shot and musketry on our position,
which after two hours, in a great measure, subsided.
About 5 P.M., they made a sudden rush on Captain
Saunders's post. One of the enemy even seized a
bayonet of one of the 84th Foot, and tried to wrench
it off through a loophole, but was instantly shot;
after a smart fusillade, which lasted for about 25 minutes, they withdrew, and gradually the fire ceased.

About 9 P.M. a third attack was made, and
was similarly repulsed; nor were these efforts confined to the places above noted. At Innes's house,
Anderson's, and Mr. Gubbins's post, large bodies of
men came forward, bringing up large scaling-ladders, several of which they abandoned. During the
day, we lost three Europeans and two sepoys killed,
and about twice that number wounded. Our garrison were under arms the entire day, the heat was
excessive, and all were greatly exhausted; nevertheless, every officer and man remained under arms
all night: after 10 o'clock all became tolerably

quiet. Captain Power, of the 32nd, who had been wounded early in the siege, died in hospital to-day, and Major Anderson, chief engineer, was reported very dangerously ill. The enemy must have had a considerable loss this day, as a great number of them were seen to fall; and we threw 150 shells, besides great quantities of round shot and grape, from which also many casualties must have occurred.

August 11*th.*—A slight alarm about 2 A.M., after which all subsided into the usual routine firing. A very fine morning; very little to be seen of the enemy, who however were not idle, as they were to-day busily employed constructing earthworks and trenches in various directions close to our position. Early in the morning the enemy fired many round shot, some of which struck the Residency, already much shattered; and about noon a very distressing accident took place. There was a high wind, and it brought down a great portion of the left wing, on the ground floor of which, in a room, six men of the 32nd were asleep. They were completely buried in the ruins. Two were got out alive after very great

exertions, but the remaining four were left under
the ruins. Immediate arrangements made for the removal of the few European women and children who
still occupied one of the rooms on the ground floor.

Major Anderson, chief engineer, died during the
afternoon. He had been ailing before the siege,
but on the commencement rallied somewhat, owing
to the excitement and novelty of the position.
Latterly he fell off again, and to-day expired; his
death no doubt hastened by the impossibility of any
change of air or diet. The look-out officers yesterday reported having seen some few doolies going
across the river with sepoys after the day of attack,
and to-day some dead and wounded were also seen
being conveyed away. The enemy were busy close
under Mr. Gubbins's ramparts, whence they had
once before been expelled by some hand grenades.
At the corner of the Seikh square also, from across
the road, they amused themselves by pushing out
over the wall bamboos with lighted straw at the
end ; but with what object was not very clear: in
the meanwhile not one of them showed themselves,
but kept well under cover. Smart firing in the

evening.   The corpse of a soldier of the 32nd was
extricated from the ruins of the Residency; three
others still remained.

August 12*th.*—A fine moonlight night.   About 3·30
A.M. the enemy suddenly commenced a very heavy
fire of round shot and musketry, which lasted for
three-quarters of an hour.   We kept close, and hardly
fired a shot, beyond throwing a few shells.   At day
light, they commenced a very heavy cannonade
and musketry fire on the Cawnpore battery; this
gradually became so sharp, that it was impossible
to work our guns, or even remain in the battery;
and we were obliged to withdraw every one but the
sentry, as the enemy's round shot had destroyed our
musketry shutters, and completely swept the battery : later in the day, our sentry, the only man in
the battery, was killed by a round shot.   This portion of our position caused us great anxiety, as we
were quite unable to hold it as it should be held;
we would not withdraw our guns, for fear of giving
the enemy confidence.   The enemy were busily
employed to-day also in digging close to Sago's

house. In order to see what they were about, at
12 o'clock a sortie was made with twelve Europeans
of the 32nd Foot under Lieutenant Chlery, accompanied by Lieutenant Hutchinson of the Engineers.
The enemy were, however, well on the alert, and
had a large covering party over their work, and as
our men appeared, they threw in such a heavy fire
that our people were compelled to retire; this
brought on a very great fire from all that side of the
enemy's attack, and they kept up a smart fire of
round shot and musketry for fully an hour, when it
gradually subsided. Finding we were unequal to
meet the enemy by a sortie, we determined to push
on our mine as fast as possible, and continue working all day and night, hoping to blow them up.

    In the evening we had as strong working parties
of Europeans as we could afford, and removed from
the Cawnpore battery, a 9-pounder which had been
disabled by a round shot of the enemy. We also
dug a trench and threw up earth on the top of
our parapets, and endeavoured to our utmost to
repair the damage the enemy had done, and make
the place as strong as possible. Several shells came

in after dusk. The heat throughout the day was excessive, and there were several fatal cases of cholera, and also several deaths among the children, who were all greatly emaciated.

In the evening, a letter to General Havelock, rolled up and put inside a quill, was despatched by the hands of an old woman; she left our position about 9 P. M., and we hoped, would be permitted to pass the enemy's sentries without being stopped. During the past forty-five days, we had sent by different hands, in a similar manner, some twenty letters, to only one of which was any reply received. The garrison, very greatly harassed and fatigued from continued exertion night and day and want of rest.

August 13*th*. — An excessively hot night. During the early part of the morning the enemy threw in a very heavy fire, which lasted for nearly half an hour, when all subsided into the usual routine firing.

Our mine near Sago's house was pushed on all night with the greatest possible speed. Every possible means was adopted by the enemy to prevent our miners working, and as only a wall and a few feet of ground divided the two parties, they resorted to squibs, rockets, brickbats, and lights at the end of bamboos, to annoy our workmen. As the latter were thrust forward with the hope of setting fire to our tiled outhouses, the ends were successively cut off by us. Several reports alive in the garrison, but on what grounds, or how stated, no one could say. However, as these were all more or less favourable to us, and encouraging to the natives, if credited, no harm was done.

Shortly before 10 A. M. the engineers reported our countermine as ready; the neighbouring outposts and garrisons were duly warned, and the mine fired, with the happiest results : the brick house in which the enemy was, and from which they had started their mine, settled down, burying all inside; the earth was thrown up to a considerable height, and only one outhouse of our own, of no consequence, destroyed. Up to the last moment, the people inside the enemy's mine were hard at work, and after the explosion the groans of the sufferers were plainly audible. In the course of the day, some few of the enemy were shot from Sago's post. In the afternoon, after several shells had been thrown in to drive as many out as possible, it was determined to go out and see what the enemy were doing near Mr. Gubbins's post. A hole being cut in the wall out of our defences, a party of Europeans, with the engineer officers, went out and found a deep trench dug through the out-houses for some distance towards our position. The work was not deemed of any great importance, and after it had been well examined, the party withdrew.

Many cases of fever to-day, and four deaths in hospital among the Europeans. Enemy very quiet during the evening; unusually so, till about 10 P. M., when they threw an 8-inch shell into our position. This appeared to be a signal; for instantly they commenced a tremendous fire with round shot and musketry, which lasted half an hour, and completely lit up the darkness around. They were busy mining us in several places, and their workmen could be distinctly heard at work. Our engineers were hard at work, trying with the best means at their disposal to frustrate their efforts; but our people were so harassed that they were not capable of any pro-longed exertion. A shaft, however, for a mine was

made in Mr. Anderson's house, and sunk to the
extent of eight feet, in view to running a sap to meet
the enemy.   Heat very great, and mosquitoes, bugs,
and fleas most troublesome.

August 14*th.* - Enemy unusually quiet all the
morning; more so than they had yet been.   Our
people were all busy preparing new sandbags, as
the old ones were so rotten, from long exposure to
the rain, that they would bear no removal: also in
countermining the enemy from out of a corner of
Anderson's house.   A Mater came in this morning,
but could give no information.   Provision for the
cattle growing short; and every means adopted to
reduce the daily consumption.   The various look-outs
reported no movement of the enemy: in a word, it
was the quietest day we had yet had.   About 4 P.M.
they began a more brisk fire.   Many cases of fever
and several deaths amongst the children.   Many
rumours abroad regarding our relieving force; but all
was conjecture.   Most of our outpost houses were
now so riddled with round shot, that it was a wonder
how any of them stood up at all: indeed most of

them were in ruins, and at Mr. Anderson's house part of the garrison had been twice pulled out of the ruins which had suddenly fallen on them; nevertheless, these posts, in spite of many casualties, were held with the same courage and devotion as was displayed the first day of the siege. At dusk we had a severe thunderstorm, with exceedingly heavy rain, which lasted for several hours, falling in a complete deluge; the night was exceedingly dark, with extremely vivid lightning. Lieutenants Fulton and Hutchinson of the Engineers went down and examined all the outhouses in Dr. Fayrer's premises, to see if any mining operations could be heard. They afterwards went down to the Buxee Khana, and examined the wall in front to some distance.

August 15th.—Heavy rain till about 3 A.M., when it cleared away, and the morning was beautifully clear and fine. The enemy fired salvos of two and three 18-pounders at once into the Cawnpore battery, and brought down all the outer wall of the house alongside it, which we used as a guard-room; making the place so hot we were obliged to

retire our men from it during the heaviest part of
the cannonade.   Lieutenant Bonham received a
severe contusion, from bricks knocked out on him
by an 18-pound shot; and later in the day the sentry
left in the front part of the battery was killed by a
round shot.   Lieutenant James Alexander was shot
through the arm while laying an 18-pounder in the
Hospital battery.   Several servants and six bheesties
of the 32nd deserted last night.   At night, advantage taken of the dark to repair as much as possible
the damage done to-day to the Cawnpore battery.
About 9 P.M. a pensioner named Ungud, who had
been sent out with a letter, returned, bringing a
letter from Cawnpore.   This was the first night
since the siege began that no burial took place.

August 16*th*. — Great progress made in our mine
out of Lieutenant Anderson's house, which had
now reached a distance of twenty-five feet from the
shaft.   Also much done in the way of making the
Cawnpore battery more secure.   Brigadier Inglis
slept in it himself.   In the early morning the
enemy fired a great many round shot, and brought

a new gun into position, to play on the corner of the brigade mess-house; also one which fired on Mr. Gubbins's post, but which was soon silenced by a 9-pounder placed in position against it. Divine service performed in the brigade-mess to a few officers who were off duty, and to the ladies. Much round shot fired during the day, but fewer sepoys in sight than usual. Every possible effort was made to curtail the expenditure of our provisions, and make them last as long as possible. The enemy threw in three 8-inch shells during the evening, and fired several round shot during the night.

August 17*th.* — The remaining portion of the Residency was deemed unsafe by the engineers, from the number of round shot that had come through it; and arrangements were made to remove the Europeans. The heat extreme, a heavy cannonade from daylight till 9 A.M., when it gradually slackened. A few round shot were fired through the Residency during the morning. Much progress was made in the mine out of Lieutenant Anderson's

house, and a new shaft sunk in the Martiniere
School, in view to running a sap towards Johannes'
house.   The Seikhs mined well, and the payment in
cash of two rupees per man for each night's work
made the work popular.   Between 4 and 5 P. M. the
enemy recommenced a slight cannonade, doubtless
stirred up by some shells which were thrown during
the afternoon.   Towards dusk the enemy threw in
several shells, and at midnight an 8-inch, which
nearly hit our laboratory.

August 18*th.* — At daylight the enemy exploded
a large mine under one of our principal posts in
the outer square, occupied by the Seikhs; the
three officers and three sentries on the top of
the house, were blown up into the air and fell
among the débris.   The guard below were all, however, buried in the ruins, and lost their lives: they
were two bandsmen of the 41st, two of the 13th,
and a sepoy of the 48th Native Infantry.   The
fficers, though much stunned, on recovering themselves ran away, and all three escaped unhurt.

When the smoke had blown away, we discovered

that a clear breach had been made into our defences, to the extent of thirty feet in breadth. One of the enemy's leaders sprung on the top of the breach, brandishing his sword and calling on others to follow; but he fell dead instantly from the flank fire of the officers on the top of the brigade-mess. Another instantly followed and shared the same fate, when the rest of the force declined making a home rush. On the first springing of the mine, our garrison was at once under arms, and the reserve of the 84th Foot (eighteen men) were immediately sent down and placed in a position which commanded the breach from the right; while boxes, doors, planks, tents, &c., were rapidly carried down to make as much cover as possible to protect our men against musketry: also a house was pulled down and a road made for a gun; and, after incredible exertions, a 9-pounder was got into a position which commanded all the breach, and was loaded with a double charge of grape. The enemy, by means of some barricaded lanes, contrived to creep up and get possession of the right flank wall of the Seikh square; but our mortar and a 24-pounder howitzer

drove the main body off, and a sudden rush
at noon cleared away the rest. We re-occupied all
the ground we had lost in the morning, and also
took possession of the houses previously held by the
enemy, and which were situated between the Seikh
square and Mr. Gubbins's house. No time was lost
in destroying them, and by sunset 400lbs. of gunpowder had cleared away many of the houses from
which the enemy had most annoyed us. By this
time the breach was securely barricaded against any
sudden rush, and at night a working party completed it. In addition to the eight men lost in the
explosion, we had this day one of the 32nd killed,
and a volunteer (M. De Prât) and three of the 32nd
wounded. Nothing could exceed the zeal with
which *all* the natives worked to secure the breach,
and make a road for a gun. The heat was fearful,
and this was one of the most harassing days we had,
all ranks being hard at work from daylight till dark,
under a dreadful sun. Lieutenant Fletcher, 48th
Regiment Native Infantry, on look-out duty at the
top of the Residency, was shot through the arm,
and had his telescope shivered by a rifle-ball, while

reconnoitring. Lieutenant Graham was also hit on the chest with a spent ball. For further accounts of the explosion of the mine, see the report of the disaster by an eye-witness, marked (II.) in the Appendix.

August 19*th.*—The enemy rather lively with their large guns this morning. Firing more particularly at the guard-rooms on the top of the brigade-mess, which were by this time well-riddled. About 2 P.M. the engineers, Messrs. Fulton, Hutchinson, and Anderson, with a small party, went out on the premises which we yesterday seized, for the purpose of blowing up some more houses and buildings. This party was supported by some Europeans and Seikhs, kept inside the square. The enemy showed nowhere, and save for a few dropping shots, their presence would not have been known.

It is worthy of notice, that even through the Pucka buildings, the enemy dug communicating trenches, probably to escape the effects of our shells; which, however, they had not always been successful in doing, as several pools of blood showed us. In the afternoon we experienced a smart cannonade, and

about dusk had a heavy shower which stayed it for
a while, and after 8 P.M. it subsided nearly entirely
into a musketry fire.

August 20*th.*—A heavy fire of musketry towards
daylight, when the enemy began the heaviest cannonade we had yet had; particularly on the Cawnpore battery, in front of which they had put another
gun in position. For three hours they fired conti-
nually, and a great portion of Mons. De Prât's
house fell in. Their round shot came in through the
Thug Jail, and enfiladed it; fortunately it struck
high, and no casualty occurred: they also threw
some shrapnel, as yesterday. Our guard rooms on
the top of the brigade mess were now entirely demolished by round shot, which came through them
almost unceasingly. An 8-inch shell went into the
Residency, and exploded on the staircase. A
soldier of the 32nd Foot was killed in the 18-
pounder battery, at Dr. Fayrer's, by a musket-
ball which struck him in the head. We were busy
all night at our mine, which was now completed, and
we hope to be able to load it and have it ready to

fire by daylight to-morrow morning. Many men were seen in the early part of the day, moving about in the bazaar (most of them sepoys). It was difficult to say what they were about, as they were moving both ways. Lieutenant Cunliffe of the artillery was slightly wounded this morning in the knee by a musket ball. Great mortality amongst the children in the garrison, and a great deal of sickness prevailed, particularly fever. All the tea and sugar for the Europeans had been for some time expended, save a small supply which had been reserved for the use of the sick and wounded. The enemy again commenced to undermine the lane running from the Cawnpore battery behind the brigade-mess, and were also engaged in some other work to the right of Johannes' house. Much firing during the evening. Captain Lowe of the 32nd Foot, had a very narrow escape; an eight-inch shell burst close to him in the trenches, and slightly wounded him in the hand, and cut off the arm of a soldier alongside him. The enemy made an attempt to burn down the gates at the Baillie Guard, by eluding the vigilance of the sentries and piling up logs of wood

and combustibles outside the gate.   It burnt fiercely,
but was soon extinguished by the water-carriers
of the 13th, without damage to the gates: the fire
was the signal for a heavy fusillade, which lasted
nearly half an hour.

August 21*st*. — At daybreak all was prepared and
ready for the blowing-up of our mine, and the simul-
taneous sortie of fifty Europeans under Captain
M'Cabe and Lieutenant Browne (divided into two
parties), for the purpose of spiking the enemy's
guns which fired into the mess house, and in
order to hold Johannes' house while the engineer
officers blew it up.   Precisely at 5 P. M. the mine,
containing 400 lbs. of powder, was sprung, and as
soon as the dust and smoke had in a measure subsided, the party ran out, drove the enemy (who were
taken by surprise, and made but a slight show of
resistance) from their guns (two), and spiked them
both, and retained possession of Johannes' house,
while the engineers made arrangements for blowing it
up.   These were soon completed, and the party with-
drawn.   A slow match was applied, and the house

laid in ruins. Our losses were one of the 84th killed, one sergeant (84th) mortally wounded, one of the 32nd dangerously wounded, one slightly wounded, and a sergeant of the artillery killed. The operation was entirely successful, and rid us of a house from which the enemy had, from the commencement of the siege, annoyed us greatly. Captain Barlow, of the 50th Native Infantry, died somewhat suddenly in hospital this morning. The grass and jungle all round had grown to a very great height, and would have given cover to a number of men to approach close up to our position unobserved. In the afternoon, a boy about twelve years of age was seen close to the Baillie Guard gate, picking up bullets that had been fired. A sepoy of the 13th on sentry-duty saw him, covered him with his musket, and compelled him to come in. An eight-inch shell fell on the top of the Residency about 9 p. m., and exploded, fortunately without injuring any one.

August 22nd.—Mrs. Green, of the 48th Native Infantry, died early this morning. There had been

also many deaths among children during the few
previous days.   Many of our supplies were entirely
expended, and the garrison were put to great inconvenience for the want of tobacco, of which for some
time past there had been none to issue.   Still more
stringent measures adopted to prevent the consumption of flour; and wheat was issued to all non-
combatants who had time to grind it.   A fine clear
night, with less musketry and more cannon firing than
usual.   Many of our defences were greatly injured
from the late heavy rain and the incessant cannonade
of the enemy.   Last night repairs were made to the
Cawnpore and Redan batteries, both of which still
required much to be done to them.   To-day an
European sentry inside the Baillie Guard gate, was
shot dead by a rifleman : the ball went through
some sand bags put up for his protection.   A sepoy
of the 13th was also hit in the knee this morning from
the same loop-hole.   Arrangements were made to
knock the place down to-morrow morning at daylight
with a 24-pounder howitzer.   Sergeant Ryder, of the
artillery, was killed dead by a musket ball to-day in the
churchyard.   Up to this date, we had lost since the

siege commenced on the 30th of June, by killed, wounded, and sickness: 101 men of the 32nd Foot, not including officers; and of the detachment of the 84th, consisting originally of fifty men, eleven had been killed and died of wounds and disease since the above date. Reports of distant firing being heard, vague rumours were afloat; but these excited little attention *now,* so often had they been in circulation, giving rise to false hopes of our reinforcements being near.

Captain Hawes, of the 63rd Native Infantry, was wounded this afternoon by a musket ball through the side and arm, while on the look-out from the top of the defences at Mr. Gubbins's post. After dark we had two eight-inch shells and several shrapnell sent in. One of the former carried off the leg of a native (who died soon after), and slightly wounded another. Repairs continued in the Cawnpore and Redan batteries. The want of tea and sugar much felt, and very large prices offered for stores of any kind.

August 23rd. — A heavy cannonade from the enemy, from daylight till about 10 P. M., when it slackened. Their principal efforts were against the

brigade-mess house and Cawnpore battery; the
former they seriously damaged, and succeeded in
entirely levelling the guard-houses on the top;
both of which had fallen in, and there was no longer
any cover for our musketry to fire from.   Our ranks
were rapidly thinning.   Two men were again this
morning mortally wounded by musketry fire.   The
enemy were busily employed in digging on all sides,
more particularly in front of the Redan; but it was
very difficult to say what their object was, as they
dug deep trenches in all directions.   Continued
reports of distant firing being heard.   The enemy
fired heavily from their guns in the afternoon, and
did considerable damage to our defences.   A working party employed after dark, making a magazine
for the powder and shells lodged in the Post-office.

We had work nightly for at least 300 men; as we
had the defences to repair daily, supplies to remove
from godowns which were fallen in from the effects
of the enemy's shot, mines to countermine, guns
to remove, barricades to erect, corpses to bury, and
rations to serve out; but with our weak, harassed,
and daily diminishing garrison, we could seldom pro-

WANT OF MEN FOR WORKING PARTIES. 125

duce as working parties more than three fatigue
parties of eight or ten men each relief; and the
Europeans were capable of but little exertion, as
from want of sleep, hard work night and day, and
constant exposure, their bodily strength was greatly
diminished. The enemy threw in an 8-inch shell
about 9 P. M. and fired all the evening. Divine service was performed at the brigade-mess in the
morning, and in the afternoon, at Dr. Fayrer's; the
sacrament was administered on both occasions.

August 24th.—This morning, at about 2 o'clock,
the enemy opened a very heavy fire, both of round
shot and musketry; commencing and concluding the
same apparently on the signal of a fireball thrown up
on each occasion. The Judicial Garrison house,
under command of Captain Germon, being in a most
dangerous state from the effects of round shot, all
the women and wounded men, also children, were
removed from that post, as well as from all the other
outposts in that quarter, into the Begum Kotee in
the neighbourhood. A sergeant of the 84th was
dangerously wounded coming up from Mrs. Sago's

house, by a sharpshooter. Lieutenant Bonham, of
the artillery, was busily employed perfecting his
arrangements for using an 8-inch mortar as a
howitzer. The experiment succeeded very well
yesterday evening.

The verandah of the Residency on the west side
came entirely down this morning. The commissariat stores in the godown underneath were removed
in the evening, as some of the arches of the lower
story were cracked, and a heavy cannonade would
have brought the whole place down. Arrangements
were made this day for still further reducing the
rations of Europeans. A kitmutghar came in from
the city last night: his account was so suspicious,
that he was placed under an European guard, as he
might have tampered with the natives. To-day we
threw two shells a long way into the city, in the
direction of the palace. The enemy tolerably
quiet; towards the middle of the day confining
themselves to sharpshooting at every one they saw
move about in our position. Mr. MacRae of the
Civil Engineer Department was very badly hit in
the shoulder this afternoon, while assisting in laying

a mortar in the Post-office; and a sergeant and a
private were badly wounded early in the day, while
going to their post. The enemy possessed many
excellent rifle shots, and fired out of their loopholes
from the houses around with great certainty; oc-
casioning us a daily loss of from three to five men.
Two sepoys of the 13th were also slightly wounded
by random shots before daybreak this morning.
Several shells came in this evening; and about
12 P. M. the enemy opened a tremendous fire on all
sides, of round shot, grape, and musketry, which
lasted for an hour: the fire was very heavy, but
they made no effort to storm, though their bugles
sounded the advance repeatedly.

August 25th.—There was the usual heavy cannonade this morning from the enemy, which continued from 5 to 9 A. M., when it slackened. All
the remaining porter in store (thirty-nine casks)
was got out of the Residency, and removed to
another place, consequent on the unsafe state of the
building; nearly one half of which had fallen from
round shot, and the remaining portion was likely

to follow. The magazine for the Post-office battery completed. In the night two sepoys of the 11th were slightly wounded by random shots. Several coolies were seen coming through the bazaar from the direction of the Cawnpore road. Sharpshooting all day long from the enemy, who had also got a new gun in position to the right of Mr. Gubbins's post. One mine completed, and three others steadily progressing ; the enemy digging on all sides.

August 26*th.* — The enemy commenced the day with a very heavy fire of round shot and musketry a little before daylight, which subsided in a great measure in about half an hour. Their earthworks had been added to during the night ; but it was difficult to distinguish new work, as the whole of our position was now surrounded with them on every side quite close up to us. A jemadar of the 71st was shot dead near the Redan this morning by one of the enemy's riflemen. The house of Innes was reported to be in a dangerous state, in consequence of the repeated round shots through it. Also reports were made of the enemy mining at the Redan. The enemy unusually quiet, and very little firing went on during the middle of the day, but they were busily employed in making trenches round us in every direction, and worked particularly hard in front of the Redan, with many coolies. No intelligence whatever. One or two servants deserted last night, and there were reports that all the servants were thinking of leaving us, unless our reinforcements arrived soon.

August 27th. — A good deal of rain during the night. A heavy cannonade from the enemy, and the usual amount of musketry fire all the morning.

To-day, the supplies of the late Brigadier-General Sir Henry Lawrence, K.C.B., were sold by auction. The brandy realised from 140 to 160 rupees (16*l.*) per dozen; beer averaged from 60 to 70 rupees (7*l.*); sherry 70 rupees; hermetically sealed hams from 70 to 75 rupees (7*l.* 10*s.*) each; a bottle of honey 45 rupees (4*l.* 10*s.*); rifle gunpowder, 16 rupees per lb. (1*l.* 12*s.*); small cakes of chocolate, from 30 to 40 rupees (3*l.* to 4*l.*); and other things in proportion. Sugar (had there been any for sale) would have commanded almost any price.

F

The enemy brought another gun into position opposite the racket court, and where we had no means
of replying to them.   A soldier of the 32nd was very
seriously wounded this morning by a musket-ball,
while sitting in the verandah of Dr. Fayrer's house.
In the evening a 3-pounder shot killed a soldier of
the 32nd and carried away the arm of another.   A
native officer of the 13th was wounded through the
foot by a musket-ball.   Our miners (working in the
gallery we had run out thirty-three feet to the
right of the brigade mess-house) heard the
enemy distinctly mining towards us.   Their sap
seemed to run for the centre of the brigade mess.

August 28th.— Heavy rain nearly all night, which
considerably injured our sap to the right of the
brigade mess, in consequence of it leaking; the rain
ceasing at daylight, we set to work, and in a few
hours got it cleared out, and had our people at work
again.   A good deal of fever prevalent, and great
mortality among the children, who faded away
rapidly from want of proper food.   A smart cannonade at daylight from the enemy, who fired hea-

vily with two guns on Mr. Gubbins's house; fortunately no casualties occurred. Last night, three men deserted to the enemy from Mr. Gubbins's post. One, a chuprassee of Mr. G.'s, took with him 400 rupees (40*l.*) belonging to different people; four servants belonging to officers also deserted.

Lieutenant Bonham fired his mortar, equipped as a howitzer, fourteen times during the day, against the new battery erected against Mr. Gubbins's post, and with considerable success, having struck it ten times; but their battery was of great strength, and required a good deal more battering to do it much mischief. We waited with impatience for the enemy's miners to break through our gallery, and were obliged to stop our own men, as the enemy left off work immediately they heard our people's pickaxe.

This night we learnt, by a letter from General Havelock, dated Cawnpore, the 24th instant, that we had no hope of being relieved for another twenty-five days.

August 29*th.*—Cooler weather. Our miners busily employed endeavouring to break into the

enemy's gallery, which, though quite close to our
own, had not yet been found.   The magazine ser-
geants at work, making an expence magazine in the
Begum Kotee.   The upper story of Mr. Gubbins's
house was no longer safe, owing to the numbers of
round shot through it, and the ladies were removed.   Much difficulty was experienced in finding
quarters for them, every place being so crowded,
and the ladies were already four and five together
in very small badly ventilated native buildings;
dreadful smells pervading the whole place, from the
half-buried bodies of men, horses, and bullocks, and
also from the drains—some of which were fearfully
offensive, as we had no means of attending to them.
Several more servants deserted last night; which
caused the very greatest inconvenience, as already
very few officers had any.   About 10 A.M. our
miners broke into the enemy's gallery, which they
immediately abandoned, and began to fill in the
shaft; we as instantly applied a barrel of powder at
the farther end of their sap, and blew up their work
altogether.   Our men brought away their lantern,
tools, and a bottle of oil, which in their haste they
had left.   Very heavy rain all the forenoon.

Sickness became daily more prevalent, and a number of officers and " the uncovenanted" were daily placed on the sick list.   To-day it was decided to issue one month's pay after the 1st proximo, for the month of July.   The heavy rain caused one of the enemy's mines, running towards the outpost called Mrs. Sago's house, to fall in.   This mine was never known to us, or even suspected.   Many and grave doubts and suspicions were entertained that the enemy were running a mine towards the Redan battery.   Lieutenant Fulton, Garrison Engineer, did not, however, share in this opinion.   A native artilleryman, who belonged to a number entertained by Mr. Gubbins, deserted from his post while on sentry over one of the guns in Mr. G.'s compound.   A European sentry fired at him, but did not succeed in hitting him.

Now that it appeared evident that the siege must last in all probability another month, increased care and vigilance in the issuing of all stores was observed.   The rain cleared off towards evening.   A considerable cannonade all through the night.

August 30*th.*— A heavy cannonade all night.   Four

half-castes (Christians) one of whom had been made a
local sergeant, and was head-writer in Captain Weston's office, deserted to the enemy; having broke
open the door in the barrier they had to defend, and
left the post unprotected. He took with him, in addition to Captain Boileau's gun, five drummers, formerly in the king of Oude's service, two drummers
of the 48th, and some ten native servants. An eight-
inch shell burst in the native hospital this morning,
killing one native and wounding two others. An
attack was expected to-day, and everything was prepared as far as possible to repel it. A good many
cases of fever. Divine service was performed at the
brigade mess at noon, and at Mr. Gubbins's house at
2 P.M., when the sacrament was administered, and
at Dr. Fayrer's house at half-past 5 P.M. To-day,
Lieut. Bonham, of the artillery, was very severely
wounded by a musket-ball, while sitting in the door-
way of the Post-office: he was a very great loss to
the garrison, having very greatly distinguished himself throughout the siege; particularly in the accuracy with which he used his mortars, and the excellent practice he had made with a mortar which he

had made to act as a howitzer. This was the third
time he had been wounded since hostilities began on
the 30th of June. Very little firing during the middle of the day, and not much movement observable
among the enemy. A European soldier of the 32nd
died very suddenly to-day ; he lost the use of his side
from sleeping in the wet trenches, and died in hospital a few hours after. Europeans and natives all
greatly distressed on account of the want of tobacco,
of which we have had none left for distribution for
a considerable time past. Great difficulty was experienced in getting shelter for women and children ;
so many houses had been destroyed by the round
shot and shells of the enemy : all suffered greatly
from being crowded together in low, small, badly
ventilated buildings. The dreadful stench which
pervaded that part of the defences held by the
commissariat officers and the uncovenanted service,
exceeded all belief. It arose from the decayed en-
trails of the bullocks and sheep daily killed by the
butchers, and of which we had no means of disposing,
but by throwing them over the defences : the decayed boosah and vegetable matter which here also

abounded, assisting in creating a stench which was
probably never exceeded. Nearly every officer who
slept at this post was laid up with fever at one time
or another; but as it was one of the weakest parts
of our defences, it was absolutely requisite that two
officers should be ever with the party occupying it.
A false alarm at sunset, and a heavy cannonade
brought the day's proceedings to a close.

August 31*st.*—The enemy fired at intervals very
hard, both guns and musketry, particularly towards
daylight. Then we found they had got another very
large gun, apparently a 32-pounder, in position under
the Lutkun Durwaza, and about 100 yards from
the Baillie Guard gates, on which it fired several
times, smashing two ammunition waggons with
which the gates were barricaded. Towards the
middle of the day the enemy were unusually quiet,
confining themselves to sharp-shooting. An excellent artillery sergeant was killed at Mr. Gubbins's
post, by a rifle-ball, which struck him in the side.

The heat excessive. In the evening, the kitmutghar of the late Captain Hayes, military secretary,

who had come in some ten days before, and was believed to be a spy, escaped from the 84th Guard
during the night, and contrived to get clear away.
He had been kept in confinement from the time of
his coming in, and had not been allowed to converse
with any one ; and therefore could give little or no
information.   About 10 P.M. the enemy very suddenly opened from nearly all their guns, and threw
in a heavy fire of musketry, which subsided in
about half an hour.   All the 13th Native Infantry
employed in making a new sunken battery to the
right of the guard-room, in order to oppose the
battery of the enemy which was located in the
Lutkun Durwaza.   Our people in the Redan battery had a narrow escape from an 8-inch shell,
which just cleared the parapet and exploded outside.

September 1st.—A fine breezy morning. Not very
much firing ; but a great deal of bugling was heard
among the enemy's troops during the early part
of the morning.   Rumours that the half-caste Christians who deserted had been murdered.   The enemy's 24-pounder fired several shots during the

morning, which took effect on the gates, smashing
them considerably.   The enemy reported to be
running another mine towards the brigade mess.

Our third sap from Anderson's post nearly completed, and considerable progress made in the one
commenced out of Sago's house.   All the boys in
garrison above ten years of age were collected and
set to work with handmills, to assist in grinding
flour for the use of the garrison.   Sickness showed
itself amongst the bullocks; and in the last two
days two bullocks had to be suddenly killed, in order
to save the meat.   This was most unfortunate, as
the stock in hand would not last (even at the
reduced rate of rations) the time we might probably
be besieged.   Arrangements were made to have
some artillery and irregular cavalry horses that
were wounded, or from want of condition were
unserviceable, turned out on this evening.   The
last cook-boy of the artillery absconded last night.
This put the men to much inconvenience, as they
had now to draw their rations with Her Majesty's
32nd Regiment; but it was better for the service,
as now there was no excuse for any of the guns'

crews leaving their batteries for their food. This
morning some fresh beef was accidentally removed
from the slaughter-yard in one of the magazine
carts. As these carts were used also for trans-
porting grain, it excited remark amongst some
Seikhs. The cart in question was immediately
marked in the presence of the Commissariat Establishment, and strict orders were given that it
should not be used again. This shows how careful
we had to be with all the natives about their castes.

In the evening, about dusk, two European artillerymen were struck in the Post-office battery by an
18-pounder shot, which killed both. Great progress was made in the battery which was erected
by the 13th Native Infantry, for the 18-pounder
to be placed in at the Baillie Guard gate. Two
8-inch shells exploded in the vicinity of our magazine, but without doing any injury. Our third
mine from Anderson's house completed, but not
charged, it being retained as a listening gallery.
Another shaft for a mine was struck out from
Captain Saunders' post, to be ready to meet the
enemy's so soon as it could be ascertained which

way they were mining. The cook-boys of two
companies of the 32nd Foot deserted to-day, which
caused extreme inconvenience.

2nd September.—Sounds of mining heard near
the slaughter-house. This was quite a new direction
for the enemy to commence this work at; but it had
not yet been ascertained for a certainty, and appeared most unlikely. Last night three men of
Her Majesty's 32nd Regiment died in hospital.

About 9 A.M. this morning a mine of the enemy
was discovered within thirty feet of Captain Saunders'
post: they came up to a well, and, not knowing
what it was, made a hole in the surface ; when the
smoke from their lamp became apparent. A countermine was immediately commenced and run out
sixteen feet, and within two feet of the enemy; it
was quickly loaded and tamped for about fourteen
feet, and the head of their gallery was blown in.
Their miners were heard at work when the hose of
our mine was ignited; and it was believed they
must have sustained some loss. Another of the
enemy's mines was also discovered this morning,

coming for the centre of the brigade mess-house;
but we had a shaft and gallery ready to frustrate
their efforts. One of the sepoys of the 13th Regiment Native Infantry was severely wounded this
morning while standing sentry. We had a heavy
cannonade from the enemy in the afternoon, and
some alteration was made in the position of some of
their guns on the Cawnpore side of our position.
The advance of a month's pay, which had been
offered to all natives, was declined by the 13th,
48th, and 71st, and pensioners, and only four
rupees each was received by the Seikh Cavalry, as
all preferred to receive it in arrears hereafter.
This spoke volumes for their faithfulness.

This evening a very sad event occurred. Lieut.
Birch, of the 59th Regiment Native Infantry, attached to the Engineer department, went out at
dusk, accompanied by four other officers, to explore
some old ruins quite close to the north side of our
position, in order to see if there were any traces of
mining. The work had been most satisfactorily
performed, and the party were returning, when a
sentry of the 32nd Regiment, who, unfortunately,

had not received the caution that a party was going
out and to be careful not to fire, seeing objects
moving in the dark outside our limits, fired his
musket; lamentable to relate, it took effect, and
the bullet passed through the lower part of the
belly of Lieutenant Birch, who died two hours
after. He was a gallant and efficient officer, and
had only been married six months. His loss was
greatly deplored by the garrison. Our miners were
all hard at work all day, countermining the enemy,
who still persevered in their efforts to blow us up.

September 3rd. — About 2 A. M. a very heavy
cannonade from the enemy till 9 A. M. Unbarri-
caded a door leading out of our position, and turned
loose during the night sixteen horses and a mule,
which had been wounded, and were unfit for use.
Further efforts made to limit the supply of flour,
and issue wheat in lieu thereof. Advances of pay
made to officers, ladies, the civil and uncovenanted
service, and a few natives who desired it.

The sun particularly powerful, and as during the
nights a heavy dew fell, and occasionally the mornings

were very cool, great fears were entertained for the health of our men; especially as nearly all had to sleep in the trenches. Consequently search was everywhere made for tents to shelter them; but the majority of these had been used as barricades and other defences, and were now, from exposure to the rain, &c., completely rotten and useless.

The enemy commenced mining at Sago's garrison, and a shaft and gallery were made to meet them. In the evening there was a heavy cannonade on Mr. Gubbins's post. A soldier of the 32nd was dangerously wounded at Innes' house by an 18-pounder shot, and another slightly wounded by grape shot. Much heavy firing from the enemy. Very severe work at mining, as our people were employed at four different points. After 10 P. M. an exceedingly heavy cannonade accompanied by musketry. The enemy were distinctly heard repairing their batteries, and moving a heavy gun with elephants, in the direction of the Cawnpore battery.

September 4th.—The usual cannon and musketry throughout the night, which greatly increased after

daylight, but gradually subsided after 9 A. M. into a
few solitary discharges of cannon.   The outer wall
of the mess house was greatly injured by the constant firing from the enemy's guns, although it was
of great solidity.   Between 9 and 10 A. M. an unusual
commotion was observable in the town, and the
streets were much crowded, for which we were
unable to account; whatever it was, the crowd
gradually dispersed, and by 11 A. M. all was tranquil,
and the enemy's guards were relieved as usual at
that hour.

Towards the middle of the day there was very
little firing from the enemy: they could be distinctly
heard in three of our listening galleries, sapping
steadily towards us.   A 32nd soldier was severely
contused to-day by a round shot, while on duty in
the Cawnpore battery, and another wounded by a
musket-ball.   About 4.30 P.M. Major Bruère, commanding the 13th Regiment Native Infantry, went
on the top of the brigade mess to endeavour to pick
off some of the enemy's gunners.   Unfortunately,
in his anxiety to get a shot at some riflemen, he
somewhat unnecessarily exposed himself, and was

hit by a rifle-ball through the chest, which almost immediately proved fatal. His death was very greatly lamented by the sepoys of the 13th, with whom he was very popular: they insisted on carrying his remains to the grave, and his funeral was attended by all the men of the 13th who could be permitted to leave their trenches. The eighteen-pounder battery made by the sepoys of the 13th, was now nearly completed, and was sixteen feet thick, besides the wall in front; the eighteen-pounder intended for it was got down, and put in position. The enemy were evidently aware of what we were about, as two shells fell quite close; one just inside, and the other outside the new battery.

The outer wall and buildings on the top of the mess house fell in this evening, with a great crash, consequent on the outer wall having been completely breached; fortunately no one was hurt, and several ladies and children still clung to the inner rooms for shelter, preferring the chance of a round shot or musket-ball to the fetid close atmosphere of an already over-crowded hovel in the interior of our position; which, after all, was perhaps hardly any safer from the fire of the enemy.

September 5th.—A fine moonlight morning. Soon after daylight, the enemy commenced the severest cannonade we had yet had. About 8000 infantry and about 500 horse were by sunrise seen moving about round our position, and evidently preparing for an attack. The garrison were soon — every man — on the alert, and remained patiently under a tremendous fire of cannon, awaiting the enemy's onset. They soon opened fire from a new battery of two guns across the river; and about 10 A.M. exploded two mines, one (a large one), close to the 18-pounder battery, and the other, a smaller one, at the brigade-mess (which we had countermined and were about to blow up.) Providentially, the enemy had miscalculated their distance in both instances, and were just short of our defences, and neither explosion did us any harm. As soon as the cloud of dust and smoke had cleared away, they advanced under cover of a tremendous fire on several points—particularly at Mr. Gubbins's post—where they came on reso-

lutely and planted an enormous ladder against the
bastion to mount it. Several reached the top, but
were so steadily received with musketry and hand
grenades, that none could gain a footing : and after
several leaders had fallen, the rest fell back to the
cover of the neighbouring houses, where they kept
up a tremendous fire. Their loss was very heavy,
as they showed themselves well; particularly in the
garden close to the brigade-mess and Sikh square,
where they fell rapidly to our rifles and muskets.
Long after the action, they could be seen carrying
away their killed and wounded over the bridges.

During the attack we only had one havildar of pensioners and two sepoys of the 13th killed, and one
soldier of the 32nd wounded (loss of hand), from
round shot. Eight sepoys of the 13th Native Infantry, assisted by three artillerymen, loaded and
worked the 18-pounder in the 13th battery, and
after three or four rounds succeeded in silencing the
18-pounder opposed to them. The sepoys were
very proud of this battery, which was entirely under
their charge, and constructed solely by them, under
the superintendence of the Engineers. A fearfully

hot-day, and a broiling sun, to which all were exposed for nearly the entire day. During last night
another shaft, eight feet deep, was sunk by the
officers of the brigade-mess as a listening gallery,
in case the enemy should run a sap in that direction.

In the evening, the enemy seemed digusted with
their want of success in the morning, and confined themselves to a few shots now and then from
their batteries. An 18-pounder came right through
the hospital from their new work across the river,
and passed through the whole length of the building, which was crowded with patients, and very
slightly wounded Lieutenant Charlton and a soldier
of the 32nd, both of whom were lying there
wounded. Passing as it did through the entire
length of such a crowded space, it was perfectly
extraordinary that this ball did not do more harm.

After all attacks, the enemy were most determined
in their efforts to carry off their dead, and generally
contrived to do so at night. To-day, as usual, the
leading men were most of them knocked over, which
greatly discouraged their followers. All reports
from positions which commanded any views of the

enemy retreating, agreed in saying that they seemed to-day more thoroughly beaten than ever.

Lieutenant James Graham, of the 4th Cavalry, shot himself through the head this morning with his revolver, in a fit of temporary insanity: he left a wife and child.

September 6th. — At 12 o'clock midnight, the garrison was aroused by a heavy cannonade from all sides, and much bugling and shouting; but it all gradually subsided in about half an hour, without any reply from our side: during it a soldier of the 32nd lost his leg from a round shot. This morning, the enemy were unusually quiet, and their guns more silent than it was remembered for a long time.

The rains seemed to have cleared off, and the sun was most powerful. Our live stock was now fast diminishing in numbers, and had any disease broke out amongst them, it would have been a most serious loss. Our stock of rum and porter was also fast running very low. Now that the stagnant water was fast drying up, the miasmatic stenches in various parts of the garrison were of a morning almost insupportable; and it was greatly feared would produce much fever and other illness.   About 1 P.M., the Engineers made a small sortie from Innes's post, and blew down a house which yesterday the enemy commenced to loophole; and which, had they succeeded in doing, would have been a most serious matter to Innes's garrison, in the present shattered and dilapidated state of the house they occupy, caused by the effects of round shot, which had steadily for the last month been fired into it from guns of heavy calibre.   Lieutenant Fulton of the Engineers was slightly contused by an explosion to-day.   About 10 P. M. the enemy sent two men with loads of combustibles, to place under the entrance gates, to set fire to them; they were seen, and one was shot dead by the sentry, on which the other fled.   An hour later, they made a very smart attack on the Baillie Guard gate, but were quickly driven back: during this affair, a very excellent native officer (a subadar), of the 13th Regiment Native Infantry, was killed in the 13th battery.

September 7th.—The enemy were unusually quiet

with their cannon this morning, contenting themselves with mining, while we as busily endeavoured
to countermine them.   An unusual commotion among
them : large numbers crossing and re-crossing the
bridge of boats; and about 11 A.M. a regiment, with
colours, and band playing, and about 1000 matchlockmen, passed from right to left of our position.
About 5000 men passed during the afternoon from
right to left; many of them seemed as though they
had marched in from a distance.   Heavy showers
during the afternoon; the garrison constantly wet.

Our miners, both European and native, were
greatly done up with their day and night exertions,
which were absolutely requisite for our preservation.
In all these operations the Seikhs and Hindoostanee
sepoys worked remarkably well.

September 8th.—Captain Simons of the Artillery,
who had been long suffering from his wounds, died
early this morning.   A tolerable cannonade kept up
all night.   The enemy had now completed a breach
in the wall enclosing the courtyard of the Martinere School, broad enough for four or five men

to pass through abreast, and which we were obliged to retrench and stockade. Nearly one-half of the officers were on the sick list, with fever and dysentery.

The shot fired in by the enemy were yesterday collected, and 280 round shot, varying in size from a 24 to a 3-pounder, were gathered from the roof of the brigade-mess alone ! In the evening we had heavy rain and a moderate cannonade.

September 9th.—During the night a shell exploded in a room occupied by a lady and some children, and though almost every article in the room was destroyed, yet all providentially escaped.

Finding this morning that the enemy were rapidly mining towards the Cawnpore battery, it was deemed advisable that our mine, containing 200 lbs. of powder, which had been ready and charged for upwards of a month, should be exploded; and accordingly, at 10 A.M., it was sprung. The effect was tremendous, and it evidently astonished the enemy, whose miners must have been destroyed. They immediately beat to arms, and opened on us from most of their batteries on that side of our position. When the smoke and dust (which were tremendous) had blown away, it was seen that the explosion had destroyed all the front face of the outhouses opposite our battery.

In the evening a body of 3000 men moved up to our right flank, which caused us all to keep particularly on the alert. About 11 P.M. very heavy rain began to fall, and the early part of the night passed away quietly. For the third time since the siege commenced there was no funeral on this day.

September 10*th.*—The rain cleared away towards morning, and all was moderately quiet till 6 A.M., from which hour till 10 A.M. an unusually heavy cannonade was kept up, and replied to by our guns and mortars. All the state jewels were brought over from the Residency, and put into the Begum Kotee for better security.

Owing to the necessity for blowing up the Muchee Bhawun, the officers brought in with them nothing but the clothes they wore. Many others in this garrison had lost everything when their bungalows in cantonments were burnt; and a few better off had shared their wardrobes with them. As time

went on, however, clothes wore out, and there were
no means of providing others; and by this time
officers might have been seen wearing the most
extraordinary costumes; few, if any, had any
semblance of a military uniform, and very many were
in shirts, trowsers, and slippers only; one gallant
civilian having found an old billiard-table cloth, had
contrived to make himself a kind of loose coat out
of it, while an officer wore a shirt made out of a
floor cloth. All carried muskets, and were accoutred
like the soldiers. At the auction of the effects of an
officer recently killed, a single bottle of brandy
realised seventeen rupees (thirty-four shillings).
The soldiers had for a month past all been out of
tobacco, and had taken to smoking dried tea and
common leaves. Not very much firing in the
evening.

September 11th.—This was a quieter night than
usual with the garrison. Much disturbance was
heard among the enemy, and the noise of elephants
was distinctly heard, as if they were moving some of
their guns into other positions. About sunrise, two
sides of Innes's house, which had been steadily can-

nonaded daily with 18-pounder shot, fell in, and the
two sentries on that side escaped with difficulty;
the post was, however, still nobly held, and preparation made for making some kind of a defence out of
the debris. Many bodies of armed men were seen
moving about, and we had the usual three hours'
morning cannonade. About 10 A.M., as our mine
out of the Seikh square (which had been charged
with 200 lbs. of powder) was ready, it was determined to explode it, as the enemy's miners could be
very distinctly heard sapping quite close; it was
very successful, completely destroying all their
excavations, and buried the party who were at work,
the groans and moans of some of whom were heard
for some time after. Later in the day, another
mine of the enemy was discovered in the churchyard. A sortie was made under Lieutenant Fulton
of the Engineers (the ground being open), and the
working party were driven off and their work
examined. It proved to be shaft and gallery, fully
five feet high, and extended twenty-four feet, running
in a straight line to the church: two barrels of
powder were separately exploded in it, and com-

pletely destroyed the entire work. Two of the enemy were shot by Lieutenant Sewell this afternoon.

At dusk, the enemy threw in (apparently from a howitzer) five hollow iron cylinders, filled with a composition (similar to that with which we are accustomed to fill our carcases) done up in strong canvas. On reaching the ground, the apparatus burst, and the five cylinders spouted forth fire without any further explosion : this, perhaps, was the most curious and complicated projectile that had yet been received by the garrison. At 7 P.M. very heavy rain, which lasted an hour and a half.

September 12*th.* — A tremendous row and noise in the city all night. A shaft sunk in the centre of the brigade-mess, in view to running a sap out across the road into the garden, in front of the enemy's battery. Rather less firing all day than usual. Very large bodies of matchlockmen were seen moving about, but a smaller proportion of sepoys. A soldier of the 32nd and an uncovenanted man were wounded; the former in the head, the latter through the hand. During the past few days no case of cholera occurred.

In the evening after dark, the 71st sepoys were employed under Lieutenant Langmore in bringing in some tents which were piled up in the Residency garden; while so employed, one of the enemy came up, evidently having mistaken our party for one of his own. He was immediately seized by two sepoys and brought in. An European sentry was killed to-day through a small loophole in the Redan, out of which he was looking, and another in the same battery was wounded during the night.

September 12th. — A smart cannonade at daylight. Considerable progress was made in our new mines out of the Cawnpore battery and brigade-mess. Captain Mansfield was seized with cholera early this morning, and died a few hours after. A great number of matchlockmen seen moving about in the bazaar. Enormous prices offered in the garrison for all kinds of supplies. A small fowl was to-day purchased by a gentleman for his sick wife for 20 rupees (2l.) A bottle of Curaçoa sold at auction a day or two ago for 16 rupees, and the same price was freely offered for two pounds of sugar. Divine

service performed at the brigade-mess, and at Dr.
Fayrer's to all who were able to attend. A man
came in about 8 P.M. from the city. He could not
or would not give any information, was looked upon
as a spy, ironed and placed in the main-guard. A
tolerably quiet evening.

September 14*th.*—A good many matchlockmen
were seen coming into the town during the day,
both over the stone bridge and the bridge of boats.
For the last two days, the bugles of the enemy had
not been heard, which led us to conclude that the
head-quarters of regiments had probably left the city.
A few doolies were seen passing down the Cawnpore
road, and a man (apparently of some consequence) was
observed haranguing a mob in the city. There was
the usual amount of firing and sharp-shooting all day.

A grievous occurrence took place in the afternoon.
Lieutenant Fulton of the Engineers, while reconnoitring from a battery in Mr. Gubbins's post, was
killed dead by a round shot, which struck him on the
head. He had conducted all the engineering operations of the siege for a considerable time previous to

the death of his chief (Major Anderson). He was a highly gifted, cool, brave, and chivalrous officer, fertile in resources, and a favourite with both officers and men. His loss was acutely felt.

September 15th.—The 18-pounder battery beyond Innes' house fired heavily, and reduced Innes's house to almost a heap of ruins; the shot came right across the entire open space round the Residency, and one soldier of the 32nd was mortally and another slightly wounded. The breach in the Seikh square made by the enemy was now tolerably retrenched. The inner square was well loopholed and barricaded, so that even if the enemy had made their way in, they would have been unable to make a lodgment. The vicinity of the houses to our defences in the outer square rendered mining easy, and we took and blew up three of the enemy's mines at this point alone. Lieutenant Fullerton of the 16th Regiment Native Infantry, died in hospital this morning.

To-day the verandah of the Residency fell in with a great crash, from the effects of the battering it had received from the enemy's 18-pound shot. This afternoon, a mortar, equipped as a howitzer (on Lieutenant Bonham's principle), was put in position against the 18-pounder battery opposite Innes's house, and fired several shots, which kept the enemy's gun in check; and one shell having blown away most of their parapet, they did not fire again from it during the evening. Under the direction of the garrison engineer, a shaft was commenced in the Baillie Guard gate by the sepoys of 13th Regiment Native Infantry, in order to run a sap out in the direction of the Lutkun Durwaza; eight feet and a half were this evening accomplished. It is intended as a safeguard, to cut off any mine that the enemy may be running towards the gateway.

September 16th. — A very sharp cannonade from daylight, for three hours. An 8-inch shell fell in the rear of the 13th battery, (for the second time since the commencement of hostilities) and mortally wounded a sepoy, and slightly wounded a subadar. Enemy were very busy erecting (apparently) a new battery, to the right of our Cawnpore battery; but it was difficult at the time to say what it was intended for: the people working at it were greatly annoyed by our shells, and it made but little progress, except during the night. They were also very hard at work in front of the Redan battery, where they had made deep trenches in all directions.

Ungud, pensioner and spy, was sent out at about 10 P. M. with a letter, done up in a piece of quill, to take to General Havelock at Cawnpore, and was promised a large reward if he brought a reply. Preparations made for getting the mortar howitzer into the courtyard in rear of the brigade-mess, by cutting a road through the intermediate walls. The mine out of the brigade-mess building, and that out of the Cawnpore battery, were worked all night, and considerable progress was made in both. The rains seemed quite over, the sun was very powerful, and much fever prevailed. Not so much firing as usual in the evening, and only one shell came in. Much bugling among the enemy during the night.

September 17*th.* — All very much as usual, with rather less firing. Many vague rumours were abroad

G

in the garrison, all without foundation. The mortar howitzer was got into position behind the brigade mess; the second shell thrown from it severely wounded two of our servants, in consequence of the shell having exploded before it cleared our defences. After the range was, however, once got, the practice was good, and several shells exploded in the embrasure of the enemy's battery. The mine out of the brigade-mess and that out of the Cawnpore battery, damaged during the day by round shot, was also repaired by a working party of sepoys from the 48th regiment Native Infantry. The sentry of the 32nd Foot, on duty at the church, had his head carried off by a round shot. Exactly at midnight the enemy made a demonstration on Saunders's post, and fired heavy volleys of musketry, but made no attempt to advance; in about half an hour, after a few shells had been thrown among them, they retired.

Many cases of fever and dysentery. Two sepoys of the 13th died in hospital of their wounds. The Seikh cavalry sowars, under Lieutenant Hardinge, worked at the barricade across the breach in

the third Seikh square, and still further strength-
ened it.

September 18*th.* — Nothing new to record.   Each
day passed away much like its predecessor, with the
same amount of cannonading and musketry fire.

Throughout the siege, a regular system of look-out
was organised from the top of the tower in the
Residency, which commanded a view of the river,
the three bridges, and the open country beyond;
and also from the roof of the Post-office, from which
a great part of the city and the road to Cawnpore
could be observed.   At the former post the officers
were relieved every two hours, and at the latter
hourly.   At each post a book was kept, in which
whatever had been observed was noted down, and
if anything unusual, or any new work of the enemy
was seen, a report of it was instantly forwarded for
Brigadier Inglis's information.   A new truck was
constructed to enable us to fit out another mortar as
a howitzer, for it would be impossible to say how
greatly we felt throughout the siege the want of
a couple of 8-inch howitzers.   To-day, the enemy

threw in (evidently from a 13-inch mortar) a piece
of wood of very great weight, which measured twelve
inches in diameter and eighteen in length! It made
a prodigious noise as it passed through the air.

In consequence of the very small stock of rum left
in store, all the Europeans were reduced to one dram
each per day. This was perhaps the quietest day of
the siege up to this date, as we had nothing but a
few stray cannon shots and a slight musketry fire
throughout the twenty-four hours.   About 11 P. M.
a very considerable noise was heard in the town,
together with much bugling and shouting.

September 19*th.*— This morning, almost before
daylight, we commenced a heavy cannonade from
the Post-office on the battery in the square house
opposite.   During the morning the enemy kept up
also a heavy fire all around; particularly on the
Residency, which now wore a most desolate tumble-
down and dilapidated appearance, from the effect of
round shot which had been steadily poured into it
daily from the commencement of the siege. About
10·30 A.M. the enemy's battery in the square house,

opposite the Post-office was set on fire by our shot, and a pretty sharp fusillade and cannonade was kept up by us to prevent the enemy from distinguishing it; the fire however soon died out. An auction was held this day in the Residency of the property (clothes, &c.) of deceased officers, and the prices that all useful articles fetched was enormous: for instance, a new flannel shirt was knocked down for forty rupees, while five old ones were sold for 112 rupees, and a bottle of brandy brought twenty rupees. A man of the 84th was shot dead at Sago's post early this morning. During the day the enemy threw into our position, probably from an enormous mortar, six pieces of wood about the size and shape of a large oyster barrel; they were thrown up in the air to an enormous height, and came down with almost incredible force.

September 20th. —At 1 A. M. a smart musketry fire and cannonade took place, which lasted for about half an hour. At daylight discovered two new batteries, which the enemy had very nearly completed, and one of which contained a 32-

pounder. We opened on them with a howitzer
and an 18-pounder, but did them little mischief;
the batteries having been made excessively strong,
with enormous beams of wood and earth. We
however, entirely prevented them from working at
either battery during the ensuing night. The
Cawnpore battery was repaired, and the centre
mine from the brigade mess was connected with the
one we had previously run out from the left. The
guard-room at Anderson's house was lowered by
digging out the floor, so as to keep the guard clear
of the round shot which passed through it; the
13th mine was also worked eighteen feet further.
A very considerable noise was heard in the city for
some hours after dark. During the day nearly as
many men as usual seen moving about. A private
of Her Majesty's 32nd at Innes' post was killed by
a round shot.

September 21*st*.—Between 12 and 1 o'clock A. M.
the enemy suddenly began a very smart musketry
fire all along the city side of our position, and opened
from their guns. We threw a few shells amongst

them, and their fire soon subsided into the usual steady fire which had gone on every night of the siege.

About 4 A.M., we had very heavy rain which lasted till about 11 A.M. The heavy rain seemed to keep the enemy quiet, and there was little firing on either side till 1 P.M., when one of our 18-pounders at the Post-office opened on the enemy's new 32-pounder battery, and knocked their parapet about, leaving the gun greatly exposed; which enabled Captain Saunders's garrison to pick off two of the enemy's gunners at the gun, and keep it silent for the rest of the day. In the afternoon, the enemy battered down a great portion of the wall enclosing the building occupied by the Martinere school-boys, and killed a water-carrier who was drawing water at the time, and who was knocked dead into the well; which was a great misfortune, as none of the natives would again use it. The body was got up soon after. Not many armed men were seen in the morning beyond the enemy's regular relief of guards and pickets. At 10 P.M. heavy rain came on. About 11 P.M. the enemy were reported to be in unusual strength near the

Seikh square, on which all were kept well on the
alert. A shell was thrown among them, but nothing
further took place.

September 22nd.—Continued heavy rain, which fell
without cessation till about 3 P.M. The garrison
were in a great state of discomfort, as little shelter
was to be had anywhere ; the roofs of all the
buildings were so injured from eighty-four days'
constant cannonading that but few could boast of a
waterproof residence. Lieutenant Cunliffe of the
Artillery, died early this morning from fever ; he had
previously been wounded. A Seikh sepoy of the
13th, a native artilleryman, two private servants,
and three grass-cutters deserted during the night;
and in the course of the morning four cook boys contrived to desert during the heavy rain. The rain did
considerable damage to various parts of our defences,
washing down many of the fascines in the batteries,
and causing several parts of the defences at Mr.
Gubbins's and Innes's post to fall down. A great part
of the outside wall of the brigade mess also fell from
the same cause. Towards evening the enemy opened

their guns, and we dismounted one of their 9-poun-
ders by a shell, which fell on the top of one of them
and killed two gunners. About 11 P.M. Ungud,
pensioner, returned, bringing us a letter containing
the glad tidings that our relieving force, under
General Outram, had crossed the Ganges, and would
arrive in a few days. His arrival, and the cheering
news he brought of speedy aid, was well-timed; for
neither our fast diminishing stores, the vague and
uncertain rumours of the advent of reinforcements,
nor the daily sights and sounds by which we were
surrounded, were calculated to inspire confidence and
check desertion among the servants and camp followers. All the garrison were greatly elated with
the news, and on many of the sick and wounded, the
speedy prospect of a change of air and security
exercised a most beneficial effect. Heavy rain fell
about 11 P.M.

September 23*rd*. — About 3 A.M. the rain cleared
off, and at 11 A.M. the sun came out and the clouds
dispersed, and gave promise of fair weather. A
smart cannonade was heard in the direction of Cawn-

pore; several imagined they also heard musketry, and the sound was listened to with the most intense and even painful anxiety by the garrison, who felt assured it must be their friends advancing to their assistance. But it was hardly expected that our force could have advanced so far, owing to the heavy rain which had fallen, and the state in consequence that the roads and country were in; however at 5 P.M. another distant cannonade was heard which lasted for half an hour, and which appeared much nearer than before : this elicited many and divers opinions, and created the greatest possible excitement.

Throughout the day, large bodies of troops with guns and ammunition waggons were seen moving about in the city, in the early part of the day to the right, and later, in large bodies to the left. In the afternoon, the enemy placed a gun in position facing down the Kass bazaar street, with what object it was impossible to say. We threw many shells into the city during the day among the parties of the enemy seen moving about. At 9 P.M. heavy rain began and fell for two hours.

September 24*th.* — Everything most unusually quiet throughout the night, and only one or two cannon shot were fired early in the morning. A considerable body of cavalry were seen moving to the right through the city, and about 8·30 A. M. a distant cannonade was heard, which continued nearly all day.

We had no news of any kind, and the anxiety of the garrison was very great. During the morning, large bodies of the enemy were seen moving through the city to the right and left. Ensign Hewitt, of the 41st Regiment Native Infantry, was slightly contused on the head by bricks struck out of a wall by a round shot. At 8 P.M. the enemy made a false attack on the Cawnpore battery, keeping up a heavy cannonade and musketry fire which lasted for about half an hour, after which all became moderately quiet. During the night guns were heard in the direction of the Cawnpore road, and the flash of them could be very distinctly seen; they were supposed to be about seven miles distant.

September 25*th*—A very unquiet night. Two

alarms, one at 1·30 A.M. and another at 4 A.M.
The whole garrison were under arms nearly the
whole night. A very great disturbance in the
city, in the direction of Mr. Gubbins's post especially. To the very great regret of the garrison,
Captain Radcliffe of the 7th Light Cavalry was
dangerously wounded while in command of the
Cawnpore battery. About 10 A.M. a messenger
came in bringing in a letter of the 16th instant
from General Outram, dated Cawnpore, announcing
his being about to cross over to this side of
the Ganges, and march on to Lucknow. The
messenger could give no account of our force,
beyond its having reached the outskirts of the city.

About 11 A.M. nearly all sound of firing had
ceased, but increased agitation was visible among
the people in the town, in which two large fires
were seen. An hour later, the sound of musketry
and the smoke of guns was distinctly perceived
within the limits of the city. All the garrison was
on the alert, and the excitement amongst many of
the officers and soldiers was quite painful to

witness.   At 1·30 P.M. many of the people of the
city commenced leaving, with bundles of clothes, &c.
on their heads, and took the direction of cantonments across the different bridges.   At 2 P.M.
armed men and sepoys commenced to follow them,
accompanied by large bodies of Irregular Cavalry.
Every gun and mortar that could be brought to
bear on the evidently retreating enemy, was fired
as fast as possible, for at least an hour and a half.
The enemy's bridge of boats had evidently been
destroyed and broken away, for many were seen
swimming across the river, most of them cavalry
with their horses' bridles in their hands.   Strange to
relate, during all this apparent panic, the guns of
the enemy in position all round us kept up a heavy
cannonade, and the matchlockmen or riflemen never
ceased firing from their respective loop-holes.

At 4 P.M. report was made that some officers
dressed in shooting coats and solah caps, a regiment
of Europeans in blue pantaloons and shirts, and a
bullock battery were seen near Mr. Martin's house
and the Motee Muhal.   At 5 P.M. volleys of

musketry, rapidly growing louder, were heard in the
city.   But soon the firing of a minié ball over our
heads gave notice of the still nearer approach of our
friends; of whom as yet little or nothing had been
seen, though the enemy were to be seen firing
heavily on them from many of the roofs of the
houses.   Five minutes later, and our troops were
seen fighting their way through one of the principal
streets; and though men fell at almost every step,
yet nothing could withstand the headlong gallantry
of our reinforcements.   Once fairly SEEN, all our
doubts and fears regarding them were ended: and
then   the   garrison's   long   pent-up   feelings   of
anxiety and suspense burst forth in a succession
of deafening cheers; from every pit, trench and
battery — from behind the sandbags piled on shattered houses — from every post still held by a few
gallant spirits, rose cheer on cheer — even from
the hospital!   Many of the wounded crawled forth
to join in that glad shout of welcome to those who
had so bravely come to our assistance.   It was a
moment never to be forgotten.

Soon all the rear-guard and heavy guns were inside our position; and then ensued a scene which baffles description.   For eighty-seven days the Lucknow garrison had lived in utter ignorance of all that had taken place outside.   Wives who had long mourned their husbands as dead, were again restored to them; others, fondly looking forward to glad meetings with those near and dear to them, now for the first time learnt that they were alone. On all sides eager inquiries for relations and friends were made.   Alas! in too many instances the answer was a painful one.

The force under the command of General Sir James Outram, G.C.B., came to our assistance at a heavy sacrifice to themselves.   Of 2600 who left Cawnpore, nearly one-third was either killed or wounded in forcing their way through the city: indeed, the losses were so heavy that they could effect nothing towards our relief; as the enemy were in overpowering force, and the position having been extended, in order to accommodate as far as possible our great increase in numbers, and the guns that were in our vicinity having been captured at considerable loss to ourselves, we remained on three-quarter rations, as closely besieged as before, until the 22nd November; when the garrison were finally relieved by the army under the Commander-in-Chief.

APPENDIX.

—⁘—

No. I.

ON the evening of the 30th May, about 9 o'clock, shots were heard at Moodkeepore (the cavalry station), in the direction of the infantry lines in Lucknow. The 7th Cavalry, consisting of about 150 sabres, immediately were turned out by their officers, and placed in three troops. On wheeling into line, about 30 men rushed out of the ranks, and rode furiously towards cantonments: they were not seen again. The corps advanced towards the race-course, towards the Residency, at a canter, which place they reached about half-past 9 or a quarter to 10. The regiment received orders to patrol round the Residency, and in the rear of Colonel Halford's house, which was done accordingly, and they afterwards formed up in rear of the lines stationed on the city road.

About 11 o'clock the 7th Cavalry marched down to the Baillie Guard, patrolled towards Muchee Bhawun,

and, finding all safe, returned *viâ* the stone bridge
through Mukka Gunge, warned all on duty at the
elephant sheds to be on the alert, and reached the Residency in cantonments about 2 in the morning. At 3
o'clock the 4th troop arrived from Chinahut, under the
command of Captain T. Boileau. At a quarter after gunfire
the cavalry marched off with the two artillery guns from
the Residency, and took up a position on the right of the
line on the 32nd parade ground. The 7th were directed
to move towards Moodkeepore, which place was reported
to have fallen into the hands of the mutineers. The
corps advanced at a canter, and on reaching the plain
close to the race-course, a large body of armed infantry,
amounting to some 1000 men, were seen advancing in
skirmishing order towards the cavalry. The report was,
as regarded Moodkeepore, too true, for the Standard
Guard was looted, public and private property destroyed,
and the 2nd Squadron standard was actually seized from
the hands of the jemadar in charge, and dashed to pieces.

Lieutenant Raleigh, who had lately joined the corps,
was brutally murdered at 5 A.M. in front of the first
troop lines. This officer was sick, and unable to join
the regiment the night before when ordered out. The
officer commanding ordered his men to form line to the
front, which was done rather sullenly; but on his order-
ing the line to take ground to the right, a number of
men broke out from the ranks, crying out that they
would charge, as their children, etc., were being mur-

dered; they rode away towards the mutineers, having been beckoned to come over by a leader riding a horse and bearing a standard. Some thirty-five or forty men left their officers. At this time an officer was sent back towards cantonments to request Sir Henry Lawrence to send up some guns, as the small body of cavalry that were left alone in front of the insurgents were in danger of being driven back.

The guns soon afterwards came up, and after a few rounds dispersed the enemy. The 7th Cavalry, in concert with the Irregulars, followed up the retreating mutineers, killed one or two, and sent in some ten or twelve prisoners. The corps returned to Moodkeepore about 10 o'clock, and marched into cantonments in the evening, and took up a position on the right of the line. Some 105 men remained with their officers up to the 12th June, on which date, by authority, they were given two months' pay, and allowed a furlough to their homes till the 15th October. The men remaining after the mutiny behaved admirably in quarters, and when told they were to go to their homes obeyed the order, quietly lodging their arms, and moving quietly homewards. The horses of the corps were marched down to the Residency at noon of the 12th, and in the evening the European and native officers, with the standards, repaired to the Baillie Guard, opposite to which the cavalry horses were ordered to be picketed.

No. II.

ACCOUNT OF THE EXPLOSION AT THE SEIKH SQUARE ON 18TH OF AUGUST.

(Dated) Lucknow, 19th August, 1857.

YESTERDAY morning, between the hours of 5 and 6, the enemy sprung a mine at the Seikh Square, blowing down the corner house, on the top of which Lieutenant Mecham and Captain Orr, with two sentries, were on the look out from the loopholes, Lieutenant Soppitt being below at the time.

A few minutes before the explosion not a single individual was to be seen in the quarter occupied by the enemy. Suddenly, however, one man was discovered by a sentry, and Lieutenant Mecham fired at him, but missed ; and immediately after the mine exploded, sending four of us, viz., Lieutenant Mecham, Band-sergeant Curtain, of the 41st Native Infantry, Drummer Ford, of the 13th Native Infantry, and Captain Orr up in the air, and burying underneath the ruins of the battery six drummers and one sepoy, i. e., Wiltshire, Williams, 13th Native Infantry, E. Curtain, A. Nugent, Rowlan, 41st Native Infantry, Fife-major Shipley, 4th Oude Irregular

Force, and sepoy Heerah Sing, 48th Regiment Native
Infantry. Of the former, I regret to state that Band-
sergeant Curtain was thrown on the enemy's side and
killed; Lieutenant Mecham and Drummer Ford were
almost unhurt, and Captain Orr escaped with a few
bruises.

Every precaution had been taken by Lieutenants Mecham, Soppitt, and Captain Orr to guard against all con-
tingencies, Lieutenant Mecham remaining at night with
the sentries, Lieutenant Soppitt and Captain Orr being
below with the guard, and occasionally visiting the sentries. Since on duty at the Seikh Battery we had already
discovered two mines, one of which we countermined,
and the other we found to be an abortive attempt at
one. The above discoveries had the effect of making us
doubly vigilant on this point.

The new mine, which occasioned the calamity of
yesterday, must have been worked by the enemy with
sharp and noiseless tools ; as—though a shaft was already
sunk beneath the battery, over which a sentry was
posted, and into which, during our respective tour of
duty, we each occasionally descended for the purpose of
listening whether mining was carried on by the enemy —
not the slightest sound which in any way led us to
suppose the same was the case, ever reached us.

There was never perfect silence in the square, owing
to the Seikhs' horses being picketed therein, the tramp-

ing of whose feet on the ground had more than once previously deceived us.

The smoke and dust thrown up enveloping us for some moments in complete darkness, and the sudden shock of the explosion, prevented my personally knowing what subsequently happened.

No. III.

DIVISION ORDERS BY MAJOR-GENERAL SIR J. OUTRAM, G.C.B.

Head Quarters, Lucknow, 5th October, 1857.

THE incessant and arduous duties which have devolved on Brigadier Inglis and his staff, since the arrival of the relieving force, had hitherto prevented him from furnishing to the Major-General Commanding the usual official documents relative to the siege of the garrison.

In the absence of these the Major-General could not, with propriety, have indulged in any public declaration of the admiration with which he regards the heroism displayed by Brigadier Inglis and the glorious garrison he has so ably commanded during the last three months, and he has been reluctantly obliged therefore to defer so long the expression of the sentiments he was desirous to offer.

But the Major-General having at length received Brigadier Inglis's reports, is relieved from the necessity of further silence, and he hastens to tender to the Brigadier, and to every individual member of the garrison, the assurance of his confidence that their services will be regarded by the Government under which they are immediately serving, by the British nation, and by Her Gracious Majesty, with equal admiration to that with which he is himself impressed.

The Major-General believes that the annals of warfare contain no brighter page than that which will record the bravery, fortitude, vigilance, and patient endurance of hardships, privation, and fatigue, displayed by the garrison of Lucknow ; and he is very conscious that his unskilled pen must needs fail adequately to convey to the Right Honourable the Governor-General of India, and his Excellency the Commander-in-Chief, the profound sense of the merits of that garrison which has been forced on his mind by a careful consideration of the almost incredible difficulties with which they have had to contend.

The term "illustrious" was well and happily applied by a former Governor-General of India to the garrison of Jellalabad; but some far more laudatory epithet — if such the English language contains — is due, the Major-General considers, to the brave men whom Brigadier Inglis has commanded with undeviating success and untarnished honour through the late memorable siege. For while the devoted band of heroes who so nobly maintained the honour of their country's arms under Sir R. Sale were seldom exposed to actual attack, the Lucknow garrison, of inferior strength, have, in addition to a series of fierce assaults, gallantly and successfully repulsed, been for three months exposed to a nearly incessant fire from strong and commanding positions, held by an enemy of overwhelming force, possessing powerful artillery, having at their command the whole resources of what was but recently a kingdom, and animated by an insane and bloodthirsty fanaticism.

It is a source of heartfelt satisfaction to the Major-General to be able, to a certain extent, to confer on the native portion of the garrison an instalment of those rewards which their gallant and grateful commander has sought for them, and which he is very certain the Governor-General will bestow in full; and though the Major-General, as regards the European portion of the garrison, cannot do more than give his most earnest and hearty support to the recommendations of the Brigadier, he feels assured that the Governor-General of India will fully and publicly manifest his appreciation of their distinguished services, and that our beloved Sovereign will herself deign to convey to them some gracious expression of royal approbation of their conduct.

Brigadier Inglis has borne generous testimony to the bravery, vigilance, devotedness, and good conduct of all ranks; and to all ranks, as the local representative of the British Indian Government, the Major-General tenders his warmest acknowledgments,—he would fain offer his special congratulations and thanks to the European and Eurasian portion of the garrison whom Brigadier Inglis has particularly noticed, but, by doing so, he would forestall the Governor-General in the exercise of what, the Major-General is assured, will be one of the most pleasing acts of his official life.

No. IV.

FROM BRIGADIER INGLIS, COMMANDING GARRISON OF
LUCKNOW, TO THE SECRETARY TO GOVERNMENT
MILITARY DEPARTMENT, CALCUTTA.

Lucknow, September 26th, 1857.

SIR,

IN consequence of the very deeply-to-be-lamented
death of Brigadier-General Sir H. M. Lawrence, K.C.B.,
late in command of the Oude Field Force, the duty of
narrating the military events which have occurred at
Lucknow since the 29th of June last has devolved upon
myself.

On the evening of that day several reports reached
Sir Henry Lawrence that the rebel army, in no very
considerable force, would march from Chinhut (a small
village about eight miles distant, on the road to Fyzabad) on Lucknow on the following morning; and the
late Brigadier-General therefore determined to make a
strong reconnaissance in that direction, with the view, if
possible, of meeting the force at a disadvantage, either
at its entrance into the suburbs of the city, or at the
bridge across the Gokral, which is a small stream inter-
secting Fyzabad road, midway between Lucknow and
Chinhut.

The force destined for this service, and which was composed as follows, moved out at 6 A.M. on the morning of the 30th of June : —

Artillery. — Four guns of No. — Horse Light Field Battery, four guns of No. 2 Oude Field Battery, two guns of No. 3 Oude Field Battery, and an 8-inch howitzer.

Cavalry. — Troop of Volunteer Cavalry, and 120 troopers of detachments belonging to the 1st, 2nd, and 3rd Regiments of Oude Irregular Cavalry.

Infantry. — Three hundred of Her Majesty's 32nd, 150 of the 13th Native Infantry, 60 of the 48th Native Infantry, and 20 of the 71st Native Infantry (Sikhs).

The troops, misled by the reports of wayfarers — who stated that there were few or no men between Lucknow and Chinhut — proceeded somewhat farther than had been originally intended, and suddenly fell in with the enemy, who had up to that time eluded the vigilance of the advanced guard, by concealing themselves behind a long line of trees in overwhelming numbers. The European force and the howitzer, with the native infantry, held the foe in check for some time, and had the six guns of the Oude Artillery been faithful, and the Sikh cavalry shown a better front, the day would have been won, in spite of an immense disparity in numbers. But the Oude artillerymen and drivers were traitors. They overturned the guns into ditches, cut the traces of their horses, and abandoned them, regardless of the remon-

strances and exertions of their own officers, and of those
of Sir Henry Lawrence's staff, headed by the Brigadier-
General in person, who himself drew his sword upon
these rebels.   Every effort to induce them to stand
having proved ineffectual, the force, exposed to a vastly
superior fire of artillery, and completely outflanked on
both sides by an overpowering body of infantry and
cavalry, which actually got into our rear, was compelled
to retire with the loss of three pieces of artillery, which
fell into the hands of the enemy, in consequence of the rank
treachery of the Oude gunners, and with a very grievous
list of killed and wounded.   The heat was dreadful, the
gun ammunition was expended, and the almost total
want of cavalry to protect our rear made our retreat
most disastrous.

All the officers behaved well, and the exertions of the
small body of Volunteer Cavalry—only forty in number
—under Captain Radcliffe, 7th Light Cavalry, were most
praiseworthy.   Sir Henry Lawrence subsequently conveyed his thanks to myself, who had, at his request, accompanied him upon this occasion (Colonel Case being
in command of Her Majesty's 32nd).   He also expressed
his approbation of the way in which his Staff — Captain
Wilson, officiating deputy assistant adjutant-general;
Lieutenant James, sub-assistant commissary-general; Captain Edgel, officiating military secretary; and Mr. Couper,
C.S.—the last of whom had acted as Sir Henry Lawrence's A.D.C. from the commencement of the disturb-

ances,—had conducted themselves throughout this arduous day. Sir Henry further particularly mentioned that he would bring the gallant conduct of Captain Radcliffe and of Lieutenant Bonham, of the Artillery, (who worked the howitzer successfully until incapacitated by a wound,) to the prominent notice of the Government of India. The manner in which Lieutenant Birch, 71st Native Infantry, cleared a village with a party of Sikh skirmishes, also elicited the admiration of the Brigadier-General. The conduct of Lieutenant Hardinge, who, with his handful of horse, covered the retreat of the rear-guard, was extolled by Sir Henry, who expressed his intention of mentioning the services of this gallant officer to his Lordship in Council. Lieutenant-Colonel Case, who commanded Her Majesty's 32nd Regiment, was mortally wounded whilst gallantly leading on his men. The service had not a more deserving officer. The command devolved on Captain Steevens, who also received a death-wound shortly afterwards. The command then fell to Captain Mansfield, who has since died of cholera.

It will be in the recollection of his Lordship in Council that it was the original intention of Sir Henry Lawrence to occupy not only the Residency, but also the fort called Muchee Bhawun—an old dilapidated edifice, which had been hastily repaired for the occasion, though the defences were, even at the last moment, very far from complete, and were, moreover, commanded by many houses in the city. The situation of the Muchee Bhawun, with regard

to the Residency, has already been described to the Government of India.

The untoward event of June the 30th so far diminished
the whole available force that we had not a sufficient
number of men remaining to occupy both positions. The
Brigadier-General, therefore, on the evening of July the
1st signalled to the garrison of the Muchee Bhawun to
evacuate and blow up that fortress in the course of the
night.   The orders were ably carried out, and at 12 P.M.
the force marched into the Residency, with their guns and
treasure, without the loss of a man ; and shortly afterwards the explosion of 240 barrels of gunpowder and
6,000,000 ball cartridges, which were lying in the magazine, announced to Sir Henry Lawrence and his officers,
who were anxiously awaiting the report, the complete
destruction of that post and all that it contained. If it
had not been for this wise and strategic measure, no
member of the Lucknow garrison, in all probability,
would have survived to tell the tale; for, as has already
been stated, the Muchee Bhawun was commanded from
other parts of the town, and was, moreover, indifferently
provided with heavy artillery ammunition ; while the
difficulty, suffering, and loss which the Residency garrison, even with the reinforcement thus obtained from the
Muchee Bhawun, has undergone in holding the position,
is sufficient to show that if the original intention of holding both posts had been adhered to, both would have
inevitably fallen.

It is now my very painful duty to relate the calamity which befell us at the commencement of the siege. On the 1st July an 8-inch shell burst in the room in the Residency in which Sir H. Lawrence was sitting. The missile burst between him and Mr. Couper, close to both; but without injury to either. The whole of his staff implored Sir Henry to take up other quarters, as the Residency had then become the special target for the round shot and shell of the enemy. This, however, he jestingly declined to do, observing that another shell would certainly never be pitched into that small room. But Providence had ordained otherwise, for on the very next day he was mortally wounded by the fragment of another shell which burst in the same room exactly at the same spot. Captain Wilson, deputy assistant adjutant-general, received a contusion at the same time.

The late lamented Sir H. Lawrence, knowing that his last hour was rapidly approaching, directed me to assume command of the troops, and appointed Major Banks to succeed him in the office of Chief Commissioner. He lingered in great agony till the morning of the 4th July, when he expired, and the Government was thereby deprived, if I may venture to say so, of the services of a distinguished statesman and a most gallant soldier. Few men have ever possessed to the same extent the power he enjoyed of winning the hearts of all those with whom he came in contact, and thus ensuring the warmest and

most zealous devotion for himself and for the Government which he served.   The successful defence of the
position has been, under Providence, solely attributable
to the foresight which he evinced in the timely commencement of the necessary operations, and the great
skill and untiring personal activity which he exhibited in
carrying them into effect.   All ranks possessed such confidence in his judgment and his fertility of resource, that
the news of his fall was received throughout the garrison
with feelings of consternation only second to the grief
which was inspired in the hearts of all by the loss of a
public benefactor and a warm personal friend.   Feeling
as keenly and as gratefully as I do the obligations that
the whole of us are under to this great and good man, I
trust the Government of India will pardon me for having
attempted, however imperfectly, to portray them.   In
him every good and deserving soldier lost a friend and a
chief capable of discriminating, and ever on the alert to
reward merit, no matter how humble the sphere in which
it was exhibited.

The garrison had scarcely recovered the shock which
it had sustained in the loss of its revered and beloved
General, when it had to mourn the death of that able and
respected officer, Major Banks, the officiating chief commissioner, who received a bullet through his head while
examining a critical outpost on the 21st July, and died
without a groan.   The description of our position, and

the state of our defences when the siege began, are so
fully set forth in the memorandum furnished by the
garrison engineer, that I shall content myself with bringing
to the notice of his Lordship in Council the fact that when
the blockade was commenced, only two of our batteries
were completed, part of the defences were yet in an unfinished condition, and the buildings in the immediate
vicinity, which gave cover to the enemy, were only
very partially cleared away. Indeed, our heaviest losses
have been caused by the fire from the enemy's sharp-
shooters stationed in the adjoining mosques and houses of
the native nobility, the necessity of destroying which had
been repeatedly drawn to the attention of Sir Henry by
the staff of engineers. But his invariable reply was,
" Spare the holy places, and private property too, as much
as possible ;" and we have consequently suffered severely
from our very tenderness to the religious prejudices
and respect to the rights of our rebellious citizens and
soldiery. As soon as the enemy had thoroughly completed the investment of the Residency, they occupied
these houses, some of which were within easy pistol-shot
of our barricades, in immense force, and rapidly made
loopholes on those sides which bore on our post, from
which they kept up a terrific and incessant fire day
and night, which caused many daily casualties, as there
could not have been less than 8,000 men firing at
one time into our position. Moreover, there was no

place in the whole of our works that could be considered
safe, for several of the sick and wounded who were lying
in the banquetting hall, which had been turned into a
hospital, were killed in the very centre of the building,
and the widow of Lieutenant Dorin and other women
and children were shot dead in rooms into which it had
not been previously deemed possible that a bullet could
penetrate. Neither were the enemy idle in erecting batteries. They soon had from twenty to twenty-five guns
in position, some of them of very large calibre. These
were planted all round our post at small distances, some
being actually within fifty yards of our defences, but in
places where our own heavy guns could not reply to
them, while the perseverance and ingenuity of the enemy
in erecting barricades in front of, and around, their guns
in a very short time, rendered all attempts to silence them
by musketry unavailing. Neither could they be effectually silenced by shells, by reason of their extreme
proximity to our position, and because, moreover, the
enemy had recourse to digging very narrow trenches
about eight feet in depth in rear of each gun, in which
the men lay while our shells were flying, and which so
effectually concealed them, even while working the gun,
that our baffled sharpshooters could only see their hands
while in the act of loading.

The enemy contented themselves with keeping up this
incessant fire of cannon and musketry until the 20th

July, on which day, at 10 A.M., they assembled in very
great force all round our position, and exploded a heavy
mine inside our outer line of defences at the Water
Gate. The mine, however, which was close to the
Redan, and apparently sprung with the intention of
destroying that battery, did no harm. But as soon as
the smoke had cleared away, the enemy boldly advanced
under cover of a tremendous fire of cannon and musketry,
with the object of storming the Redan. But they were
received with such a heavy fire, that after a short
struggle they fell back with much loss. A strong
column advanced at the same time to attack Innes' post,
and came on to within ten yards of the palisades, afford-
ing to Lieutenant Loughnan, 13th Native Infantry, who
commanded the position, and his brave garrison, composed of gentlemen of the Uncovenanted Service, a few of
Her Majesty's 32nd Foot and the 13th Native Infantry,
an opportunity of distinguishing themselves, which they
were not slow to avail themselves of, and the enemy
were driven back with great slaughter. The insurgents
made minor attacks at almost every outpost, but were
invariably defeated, and at 2 P.M. they ceased their
attempts to storm the place, although their musketry fire
and cannonading continued to harass us unceasingly as
usual. Matters proceeded in this manner until the 10th
August, when the enemy made another assault, having previously sprung a mine close to the brigade mess, which en-

tirely destroyed our defences for the space of twenty feet,
and blew in a great portion of the outside wall of the
house occupied by Mr. Shilling's garrison.   On the dust
clearing away, a breach appeared, through which a regiment could have advanced in perfect order, and a few of
the enemy came on with the utmost determination, but
were met with such a withering flank fire of musketry
from the officers and men holding the top of the brigade
mess, that they beat a speedy retreat, leaving the
more adventurous of their numbers lying on the crest of
the breach.   While this operation was going on, another
large body advanced on the Cawnpore battery, and succeeded in locating themselves for a few minutes in the
ditch.   They were, however, dislodged by hand-grenades.
At Captain Anderson's post they also came boldly forward
with scaling ladders, which they planted against the wall;
but here, as elsewhere, they were met with the most indomi-
table resolution, and the leaders being slain, the rest fled,
leaving the ladders, and retreated to their batteries and
loopholed defences, from whence they kept up, for the rest
of the day, an unusually heavy cannonade and musketry
fire.   On the 18th August the enemy sprung another
mine in front of the Sikh lines with very fatal effect.
Captain Orr (unattached), Lieutenants Mecham and
Soppitt, who commanded the small body of drummers
composing the garrison, were blown into the air; but
providentially returned to earth with no further injury

than a severe shaking. The garrison, however, were not so fortunate. No less than eleven men were buried alive under the ruins, from whence it was impossible to extricate them, owing to the tremendous fire kept up by the enemy from houses situated not ten yards in front of the breach. The explosion was followed by a general assault of a less determined nature than the two former efforts, and the enemy were consequently repulsed without much difficulty. But they succeeded, under cover of the breach, in establishing themselves in one of the houses in our position, from which they were driven in the evening by the bayonets of Her Majesty's 32nd and 84th Foot. On the 5th of September the enemy made their last serious assault. Having exploded a large mine, a few feet short of the bastion of the 18-pounder gun, in Major Apthorp's post, they advanced with large heavy scaling ladders, which they planted against the wall, and mounted, thereby gaining for an instant the embrasure of a gun. They were, however, speedily driven back with loss by hand-grenades and musketry. A few minutes subsequently they sprung another mine close to the brigade mess, and advanced boldly; but soon the corpses strewed in the garden in front of the post bore testimony to the fatal accuracy of the rifle and musketry fire of the gallant members of that garrison, and the enemy fled ignominiously, leaving their leader—a fine-looking old native officer—among the slain. At other posts they

made similar attacks, but with less resolution, and everywhere with the same want of success. Their loss upon
this day must have been very heavy, as they came on
with much determination, and at night they were seen
bearing large numbers of their killed and wounded over
the bridges in the direction of cantonments.

The above is a faint attempt at a description of the four
great struggles which have occurred during this protracted season of exertion, exposure, and suffering. His
Lordship in Council will perceive that the enemy invariably commenced his attacks by the explosion of a mine,—
a species of offensive warfare, for the exercise of which
our position was unfortunately peculiarly situated; and
had it not been for the most untiring vigilance on our
part, in watching and blowing up their mines before they
were completed, the assaults would probably have been
much more numerous, and might, perhaps, have ended in
the capture of the place. But by countermining in all
directions, we succeeded in detecting and destroying no
less than four of the enemy's subterraneous advances
towards important positions, two of which operations were
eminently successful, as on one occasion not less than
eighty of them were blown into the air, and twenty
suffered a similar fate on the second explosion. The
labour, however, which devolved upon us in making
these counter-mines, in the absence of a body of skilled
miners, was very heavy. The Right Honourable the

Governor-General in Council will feel that it would be impossible to crowd, within the limits of a despatch, even the principal events, much more the individual acts of gallantry, which have marked this protracted struggle. But I can conscientiously declare my conviction, that few troops have ever undergone greater hardships, exposed as they have been to a never-ceasing musketry fire and cannonade. They have also experienced the alternate vicissitudes of extreme wet and intense heat, and that too with very insufficient shelter from either, and in many places without any shelter at all. In addition to having to repel real attacks, they have been exposed night and day to the hardly less harassing false alarms which the enemy have been constantly raising. The insurgents have frequently fired very heavily, sounded the advance, and shouted for several hours together, though not a man could be seen, with the view, of course, of harassing our small and exhausted force; in which object they succeeded, for no part has been strong enough to allow of a portion only of the garrison being prepared in the event of a false attack being turned into a real one. All, therefore, had to stand to their arms, and to remain at their posts until the demonstration had ceased; and such attacks were of almost nightly occurrence. The whole of the officers and men have been on duty night and day during the eighty-seven days which the siege had lasted, up to the arrival of Sir J. Outram, G.C.B.

In addition to this incessant military duty, the force
has been nightly employed in repairing defences, in
moving guns, in burying dead animals, in conveying ammunition and commissariat stores from one place to
another, and in other fatigue duties too numerous and too
trivial to enumerate here. I feel, however, that any
words of mine will fail to convey any adequate idea of
what our fatigue and labours have been—labours in
which all ranks and all classes, civilians, officers, and
soldiers, have all borne an equally noble part. All have
together descended into the mine; all have together
handled the shovel for the interment of the putrid bullock; and all, accoutred with musket and bayonet, have
relieved each other on sentry, without regard to the dis-
tinctions of rank, civil or military. Notwithstanding all
these hardships, the garrison has made no less than five
sorties, in which they spiked two of the enemy's heaviest
guns, and blew up several of the houses from which they
had kept up the most harassing fire. Owing to the
extreme paucity of our numbers, each man was taught to
feel that on his own individual efforts alone depended in
no small measure the safety of the entire position. This
consciousness incited every officer, soldier, and man to
defend the post assigned to him with such desperate
tenacity, and fight for the lives which Providence had
intrusted to his care with such dauntless determination,
that the enemy, despite their constant attacks, their heavy

mines, their overwhelming numbers, and their incessant fire, could never succeed in gaining one inch of
ground within the bounds of this straggling position,
which was so feebly fortified, that had they once obtained
a footing in any of the outposts, the whole place must
inevitably have fallen.

If further proof be wanting of the desperate nature of
the struggle which we have, under God's blessing, so long
and so successfully waged, I would point to the roofless and
ruined houses, to the crumpled walls, to the exploded mines,
to the open breaches, to the shattered and disabled guns
and defences, and lastly to the long and melancholy list of
the brave and devoted officers and men who have fallen.
These silent witnesses bear sad and solemn testimony to
the way in which this feeble position has been defended.
During the early part of these vicissitudes, we were
left without any information whatever regarding the
posture of affairs outside.   An occasional spy did indeed
come in with the object of inducing our sepoys and servants to desert ; but the intelligence derived from such
sources was, of course, entirely untrustworthy.   We sent
our messengers, daily calling for aid and asking for information, none of whom ever returned until the 26th
day of the siege, when a pensioner named Ungud
came back with a letter from General Havelock's camp,
informing us that they were advancing with a force
sufficient to bear down all opposition, and would be with

us in five or six days. A messenger was immediately
despatched, requesting that on the evening of their arrival
on the outskirts of the city, two rockets might be sent
up, in order that we might take the necessary measures
for assisting them in forcing their way in.   The sixth
day, however, expired, and they came not ; but for many
evenings after officers and men watched for the ascension
of the expected rockets, with hopes such as make the
heart sick.   We knew not then, nor did we learn until
the 29th of August — or thirty-five days later — that the
relieving force, after having fought most nobly to effect
our deliverance, had been obliged to fall back for reinforcements, and this was the last communication we
received until two days before the arrival of Sir James
Outram on Sept. 25th.

Besides heavy visitations of cholera and smallpox, we
have also had to contend against a sickness which has
almost universally pervaded the garrison.   Commencing
with a very painful eruption it has merged into a low
fever, combined with diarrhœa ; and although few or no
men have actually died from its effects, it leaves behind a
weakness and lassitude which, in the absence of all mate-
rial sustenance, save coarse beef and still coarser flour,
none have been able entirely to get over.   The mortality
among the women and children, and especially among the
latter, from these diseases and from other causes, has been
perhaps the most characteristic of the siege.   The want

of native servants has also been a source of much privation. Owing to the suddenness with which we were
besieged, many of these people who might perhaps have
otherwise proved faithful to their employers, but who
were outside of the defences at the time, were altogether
excluded. Very many more deserted, and several fami-
lies were consequently left without the services of a single
domestic. Several ladies have had to tend their children,
and even to wash their own clothes, as well as to cook
their scanty meals entirely unaided. Combined with the
absence of servants, the want of proper accommodation
has probably been the cause of much of the disease with
which we have been afflicted. I cannot refrain from
bringing to the prominent notice of his Lordship in Council the patient endurance and the Christian resignation
which have been evinced by the women of this garrison.
They have animated us by their example. Many, alas!
have been made widows and their children fatherless in
this cruel struggle. But all such seem resigned to the
will of Providence, and many, among whom may be mentioned the honoured names of Birch, of Polehampton, of
Barbor, and of Gall, have, after the example of Miss
Nightingale, constituted themselves the tender and soli-
citous nurses of the wounded and dying soldiers in the
hospital.

It only remains for me to bring to the favourable notice
of his Lordship in Council the names of those officers

who have most distinguished themselves, and afforded me
the most valuable assistance in these operations. Many of
the best and bravest of these now rest from their labours.
Among them are Lieutenant-Colonel Case and Captain
Radcliffe, whose services have already been narrated.
Captain Francis, 13th Native Infantry — who was killed
by a round shot — had particularly attracted the attention
of Sir H. Lawrence for his conduct while in command of
the Muchee Bhawun; Captain Fulton, of the Engineers,
who also was struck by a round shot, had, up to the time
of his early and lamented death, afforded me the most invaluable aid; he was indeed indefatigable; Major Anderson, the chief Engineer, though, from the commencement of the siege, incapable of physical exertion from the
effects of the disease under which he eventually sank,
merited my warm acknowledgments for his able counsel.
Captain Simons, commandant of artillery, distinguished
himself at Chinhut, where he received the two wounds
which ended in his death; Lieutenants Shepherd and
Arthur, 7th Light Cavalry, who were killed at their
posts; Captain Hughes, 57th Native Infantry, who was
mortally wounded at the capture of a house which formed
one of the enemy's outposts; Captain M'Cabe, of the
32nd Foot, who was killed at the head of his men while
leading his fourth sortie, as well as Captain Mansfield, of
the same corps, who died of cholera—were all officers who
had distinguished themselves highly. Mr. Lucas too, a
gentleman volunteer, and Mr. Boyson, of the Uncove-

nanted Service — who fell when on the look-out at one
of the most perilous outposts — had earned themselves
reputations for coolness and gallantry.

The officers who commanded outposts — Lieutenant-
Colonel Master, 7th Light Cavalry; Major Apthorp,
and Captain Sanders, 41st Native Infantry; Captain
Boileau, 7th Light Cavalry; Captain Germon, 13th
Native Infantry; Lieutenant Aitkin, and Lieutenant
Loughnan, of the same corps; Captain Anderson, 25th
Native Infantry; Lieutenant Graydon, 44th Native
Infantry; Lieutenant Langmore, 71st Native Infantry;
and Mr. Schilling, principal of the Martinière College —
have all conducted ably the duties of their onerous
position.   No further proof of this is necessary than the
fact which I have before mentioned, that throughout the
whole duration of the siege, the enemy were not only
unable to take, but they could not even succeed in
gaining, one inch of the posts commanded by these gallant
gentlemen.   Colonel Master commanded the critical and
important post of the brigade mess, on either side of
which was an open breach, only flanked by his handful
of riflemen and musketeers.   Lieutenant Aitkin, with the
whole of the 13th Native Infantry, which remained to us
with the exception of their Sikhs, commanded the Baillie
Guard — perhaps the most important position in the
whole of the defences; and Lieutenant Langmore, with
the remnant of his regiment (the 71st), held a very ex

posed position between the Hospital and the Water
Gate.   This gallant and deserving young soldier and his
men were entirely without shelter from the weather, both
by night and by day.

My thanks are also due to Lieutenants Anderson,
Hutchinson, and Innes, of the Engineers, as well as
Lieutenant Tulloch, 58th Native Infantry, and Lieutenant Hay, 48th Native Infantry, who were placed under
them to aid in the arduous duties devolving upon that
department.   Lieutenant Thomas, Madras Artillery, who
commanded that arm of the service for some weeks, and
Lieutenants Macfarlane and Bonham, rendered me the
most effectual assistance.   I was, however, deprived of
the services of the two latter, who were wounded,
Lieutenant Bonham no less than three times, early in the
siege.   Captain Evans, 17th Bengal Native Infantry, who,
owing to the scarcity of artillery officers, was put in
charge of some guns, was ever to be found at his post.

Major Lowe, commanding Her Majesty's 32nd Regiment; Captain Bassano, Lieutenants Lawrence, Edmonstoune, Foster, Harmar, Cooke, Clery, Browne, and
Charlton, of that corps, have all nobly performed their
duty.   Every one of these officers, with the exception of
Lieutenants Lawrence and Clery, have received one or
more wounds of more or less severity.   Quartermaster
Stribbling, of the same corps, also conducted himself to
my satisfaction.

Captain O'Brien, Her Majesty's 84th Foot; Captain

Kemble, 41st Native Infantry; Captain Edgell, 53rd Native Infantry; Captain Dinning, Lieutenant Sewell, and Lieutenant Worsley, of the 71st Native Infantry; Lieutenant Warner, 7th Local Corps; Ensign Ward, 48th Native Infantry (who, when most of our artillery officers were killed or disabled, worked the mortars with excellent effect); Lieutenant Graham, 11th Native Infantry; Lieutenant Mecham, 4th Oude Locals; and Lieutenant Keir, 41st Native Infantry, have all done good and willing service throughout the siege, and I trust that they will receive the favourable notice of his Lordship in Council.

I beg particularly to call the attention of the Government of India to the untiring industry, the extreme devotion, and the great skill which have been evinced by Surgeon Scott (superintending surgeon), and Assistant-surgeon Boyd, of Her Majesty's 32nd Foot; Assistant-surgeon Bird, of the Artillery; Surgeon Campbell, 7th Light Cavalry; Surgeon Brydon, 7th Native Infantry; Surgeon Ogilvie, sanitary commissioner; Assistant-surgeon Fayrer, civil surgeon; Assistant-surgeon Partridge, 2nd Oude Irregular Cavalry; Assistant-surgeon Greenhow; Assistant-surgeon Darby, and by Mr. Apothecary Thompson, in the discharge of their onerous and most important duties.

Messrs. Thornhill and Capper, of the Civil Service, have been both wounded, and the way in which they, as well as Mr. Martin, the deputy commissioner of Lucknow, conducted themselves, entitles them to a place in this despatch. Captain Carnegie, the special assistant com-

missioner, whose invaluable service previous to the commencement of the siege I have frequently heard warmly
dilated upon, both by Sir H. Lawrence and by Major Banks,
and whose exertions will probably be more amply brought
to notice by the civil authorities on some future occasion,
has conducted the office of provost marshal to my satisfaction.   The Reverend Mr. Harris and the Reverend
Mr. Polehampton, assistant chaplains, vied with each
other in their untiring care and attention to the suffering
men.   The latter gentleman was wounded in the hospital,
and subsequently unhappily died of cholera.   Mr. M'Crae,
of the Civil Engineers, did excellent service, at the guns,
until he was severely wounded.   Mr. Cameron, also, a
gentleman who had come to Oude to inquire into the
resources of the country, acquired the whole mystery of
mortar practice, and was of the most signal service until
incapacitated by sickness.   Mr. Marshall, of the road
department, and other members of the Uncovenanted
Service, whose names will, on a subsequent occasion, be
laid before the Government of India, conducted themselves bravely and steadily.   Indeed, the entire body of
these gentlemen have borne themselves well, and have
evinced great coolness under fire.

I have now only to bring to the notice of the Right
Honourable the Governor-General in Council the conduct of the several officers who composed my staff: —
Lieutenant James, sub-assistant commissary-general, was
severely wounded by a shot through the knee at Chin-

hut, notwithstanding which he refused to go upon the sick list, and carried on his most trying duties throughout the entire siege. It is not too much to say that the garrison owe their lives to the exertions and firmness of this officer. Before the struggle commenced, he was ever in the saddle, getting in supplies, and his untiring vigilance in their distribution after our difficulties had begun, prevented a waste which otherwise, long before the expiration of the eighty-seven days, might have annihilated the force by the slow process of starvation.

Captain Wilson, 13th Native Infantry, officiating deputy-assistant adjutant-general, was ever to be found where shot was flying thickest; and I am at a loss to decide whether his services were more invaluable owing to the untiring physical endurance and bravery which he displayed, or to his ever-ready and pertinent counsel and advice in moments of difficulty and danger.

Lieutenant Hardinge, an officer whose achievements and antecedents are well known to the Government of India, has earned fresh laurels by his conduct throughout the siege. He was officiating as deputy-assistant quartermaster-general, and also commanded the Sikh portion of the cavalry of the garrison. In both capacities his services have been invaluble, especially in the latter, for it was owing alone to his tact, vigilance, and bravery, that the Sikh horsemen were induced to persevere in holding a very unprotected post under a heavy fire.

Lieutenant Barwell, 71st Native Infantry, the fort ad-

jutant and officiating major of brigade, has proved himself
to be an efficient officer.

Lieutenant Birch, of the 71st Native Infantry, has
been my aide-de-camp throughout the siege. I firmly
believe there never was a better aide-de-camp. He has
been indefatigable, and ever ready to lead a sortie, or to
convey an order to a threatened outpost under the heaviest
fire. On one of these occasions he received a slight wound
on the head. I beg to bring the services of this most
promising and intelligent young officer to the favourable
consideration of his Lordship in Council.

I am also much indebted to Mr. Cooper, Civil Service,
for the assistance he has on many occasions afforded me
by his judicious advice. I have, moreover, ever found
him most ready and willing in the performance of the
military duties assigned to him, however exposed the post
or arduous the undertaking. He commenced his career
in Her Majesty's service, and consequently had had some
previous experience of military matters. If the road to
Cawnpore had been made clear by the advent of our
troops, it was my intention to have deputed this officer to
Calcutta, to detail in person the occurrences which have
taken place, for the information of the Government of
India. I still hope that when our communications shall
be once more unopposed he may be summoned to Calcutta
for this purpose.

Lastly, I have the pleasure of bringing the splendid
behaviour of the soldiers, viz., the men of Her Majesty's

32nd Foot, the small detachment of Her Majesty's 84th
Foot, the European and Native Artillery, the 13th, 48th,
and 71st Regiments of Native Infantry, and the Sikhs
of the respective corps, to the notice of the Government
of India. The losses sustained by Her Majesty's 32nd,
which is now barely 300 strong ; by Her Majesty's 84th,
and by the European Artillery, show at least that they
knew how to die in the cause of their countrymen.
Their conduct under the fire, the exposure, and the
privations which they had to undergo, has been throughout most admirable and praiseworthy.

As another instance of the desperate character of our
defence, and the difficulties we have had to contend with,
I may mention that the number of our artillerymen was
so reduced that on the occasion of an attack, the gunners,
aided as they were by men of Her Majesty's 32nd Foot,
and by volunteers of all classes, had to run from one
battery to another, wherever the fire of the enemy was
hottest, there not being nearly enough men to serve half
the number of guns at the same time. In short, at last,
the number of European gunners was only twenty-four,
while we had, including mortars, no less than thirty guns
in position.

With respect to the native troops, I am of opinion that
their loyalty has never been surpassed. They were indifferently fed and worse housed. They were exposed—
especially the 13th Regiment—under the gallant Lieutenant Aitken, to a most galling fire of round shot and

musketry, which materially decreased their numbers.
They were so near the enemy that conversation could be
carried on between them; and every effort, persuasion,
promise, and threat was alternately resorted to, in vain, to
seduce them from their allegiance to the handful of Europeans, who, in all probability, would have been sacrificed
by their desertion.   All the troops behaved nobly, and
the names of those men of the native force who have particularly distinguished themselves, have been laid before
Major-General Sir James Outram, G.C.B., who has
promised to promote them.   Those of the European force
will be transmitted in due course for the orders of His
Royal Highness the General Commanding-in-Chief.

In conclusion, I beg leave to express, on the part of
myself and the members of this garrison, our deep and
grateful sense of the conduct of Major-General Sir J.
Outram, G.C.B.; of Brigadier-General Havelock, C.B.,
and of the troops under those officers who so de-
votedly came to our relief at so heavy a sacrifice of life.
We are also repaid for much suffering and privation by
the sympathy which our brave deliverers say our perilous
and unfortunate position has excited for us in the hearts
of our countrymen throughout the length and breadth of
Her Majesty's dominions.—I have, &c.,

(Signed)   T. Inglis,

Colonel, Her Majesty's 32nd, Brigadier.

No. V.

From the Homeward Mail.

A COMPLETE NOMINAL LIST OF THE OFFICERS, MEMBERS
OF THE UNCOVENANTED SERVICE, AND WOMEN AND
CHILDREN OF THE LUCKNOW GARRISON ; AND AS THE
RETURN PROCEEDED FROM AN OFFICIAL SOURCE THE
AUTHENTICITY MAY BE FULLY RELIED ON.

General Staff.

Brigadier-General Sir H. M. Lawrence, chief commissioner, killed ; Lieutenant Hutchinson, aide-de-camp ;
Captain Hayes, military secretary, killed; Captain Edgell,
officiating; Captain Wilson, deputy assistant-adjutant-
general, contused, recovered ; Lieutenant Hardinge, deputy assistant quartermaster-general, twice wounded, recovered ; Lieutenant James, sub-assistant commissary
general, wounded, doing well ; Major Anderson, chief
engineer, dead ; Major Marriott, pension-paymaster.

Brigade Staff.

Brigadier Handscomb, commanding Oude brigade,
killed; Brigadier Inglis, commanding the garrison; Lieutenant Birch, aide-de-camp, slightly wounded, recovered ;

Lieutenant Barwell, town and fort adjutant, officiating major of brigade; Captain Carnegie, provost marshal.

Artillery.

Captain Simons, wounded, since dead; First Lieutenant Alexander, wounded, recovered, since killed; First Lieutenant Thomas (Madras); Second Lieutenant Lewin, killed; Lieutenant Brice, wounded, since dead; Second Lieutenant Bonham, wounded three times, doing well; Second Lieutenant J. Alexander, slightly wounded, recovered; Second Lieutenant MacFarlan, wounded, doing well; Second Lieutenant Cunliffe, wounded, since dead.

Engineers.

Captain Fulton, garrison engineer, killed; Lieutenant Anderson (Madras) officiating; Lieutenant Innes.

7th Regiment Light Cavalry.

Lieutenant-Colonel Master; Captain Staples, killed; Captain Radcliffe, wounded, since dead; Captain Boileau, slightly wounded, recovered; Lieutenant Arthur, killed; Lieutenant Boulton, killed; Lieutenant Warner, adjutant; Lieutenant Martin, killed; Lieutenant Farquhar, wounded, convalescent; Lieutenant Raleigh, killed; Surgeon Campbell; veterinary surgeon Hely, killed; riding master Eldridge, killed.

Her Majesty's 32nd Foot.

Lieutenant-Colonel Case, killed ; Major Lowe, commanding, twice wounded, doing well; Captain Stevens, killed; Captain Mansfield, dead; Captain Power, wounded, since dead ; Captain Bassano, wounded, recovered ; Captain M'Cabe, mortally wounded, since dead ; Lieutenant Lawrence; Lieutenant Edmonstoune, twice wounded, doing well ; Lieutenant Webb, killed; Lieutenant Foster, wounded, recovered ; Lieutenant Clery, Lieutenant Brown, Lieutenant Brackenbury, killed ; Lieutenant Harmer, wounded, doing well; Lieutenant Cook, slightly wounded, recovered ; Ensign Charlton, wounded, doing well ; Ensign Studdy, killed ; Paymaster Giddings, Quartermaster Stribbling ; Surgeon Scott, M.D. ; Assistant-Surgeon Boyd.

Detachment of Her Majesty's 84th Foot.

Lieutenant O'Brien, wounded, recovered ; Ensign McGrath.

13th Regiment Native Infantry.

Major Bruère, killed; Captain Waterman, wounded ; recovered ; Captain Germon, Captain Francis, killed ; Lieutenant Aitken, Quartermaster, Lieutenant Chambers, adjutant, wounded, doing well ; Lieutenant Thain, Lieutenant Loughnan, Ensign Green, dead ; Surgeon Pitt.

41*st Regiment Native Infantry.*

Major Apthorp; Captain Kemble, wounded, recovered; Captain Sanders; Lieutenant Ruggles; Lieutenant Graves, dead; Lieutenant Darrah; Lieutenant Inglis, wounded, recovered; Lieutenant Keir; Ensign McGregor, dead; Ensign Hewitt, slightly wounded, recovered; Surgeon Macdonald, dead.

48*th Regiment Native Infantry.*

Lieutenant-Colonel Palmer; Major Bird; Captain Burmester, killed; Captain Green; Lieutenant Huxham, twice wounded, doing well; Lieutenant Smith, Adjutant, wounded (accidentally), doing well; Lieutenant Ouseley, Quarter-master; Lieutenant Fletcher, wounded, doing well; Lieutenant Dashwood, wounded, since dead; Lieutenant Hay, wounded slightly, recovered; Ensign Farquharson, killed; Ensign O'Dowda, slightly wounded, recovered; Ensign Ward; Surgeon Wells, wounded slightly, recovered.

71*st Regiment Native Infantry.*

Colonel Halford, dead; Captain Strangways, slightly wounded, recovered; Captain Dinning; Captain Maclean, killed; Lieutenant Langmore, Adjutant; Lieutenant Sewell; Lieutenant Grant, killed; Ensign Worsley, Ensign C. W. Campbell, wounded, doing well; Ensign W. Campbell; Surgeon Brydon, wounded, recovered.

Officers not belonging to the Oude Brigade.

Major Banks, Provisional Chief Commissioner, killed; Captain Stuart, 3rd Native Infantry; Lieutenant Fullerton, 44th Native Infantry, dead; Lieutenant Lester, 32nd Native Infantry, killed; Lieutenant Tullock, 58th Native Infantry; Lieutenant Birch, 59th Native Infantry, killed; Ensign Inglis, 63rd Native Infantry, doing duty 13th Native Infantry; Captain Weston, 65th Native Infantry, Oude Frontier Police; Ensign Dashwood, 18th Native Infantry, mortally wounded, since dead.

Oude Irregular Force.

Brigadier Gray, Commanding; Captain Barlow, Major of Brigade, wounded, since dead; Captain Forbes, 1st Oude Cavalry, slightly wounded, recovered; Lieutenant Bax, Second in Command, killed; Lieutenant Graham, Officiating Adjutant, dead; Assistant-Surgeon Greenhow; Major Gall, 2nd Oude Cavalry, killed; Lieutenant Shepherd, Second in Command, killed; Lieutenant Barbor, Adjutant, killed; Gentleman Volunteer Fayrer, killed; Assistant-Surgeon Partridge; Lieutenant Graham, Adjutant, 3rd Oude Cavalry, slightly wounded twice, recovered; Lieutenant Clarke, 1st Oude Infantry; Captain Hughes, 4th Oude Infantry, wounded, since dead; Lieutenant Soppitt, 4th Oude Infantry; Assistant-Surgeon Hadow; Captain Hawes, 6th Oude Infantry,

wounded, recovered; Lieutenant Grant, Second in Com-
mand, wounded, since dead; Apothecary Thompson;
Lieutenant Graydon, 7th Oude Infantry, very dan-
gerously wounded, since dead; Lieutenant Watson, Se-
cond in Command; Lieutenant Mechamns, Adjutant;
Lieutenant Vanrenen, 9th Oude Infantry; Assistant-
Surgeon Darby, M.D., 10th Oude Infantry; Captain
Hearsey, unattached; Captain Orr, unattached.

Assistant Chaplains of Lucknow.

The Reverend H. P. Harris; the Reverend H. S. Polehampton, wounded, since dead.

Civil Surgeons.

Surgeon Ogilvie, Superintendent of Jails; Assistant-
Surgeon Fayrer, Residency Surgeon.

Gentlemen of the Civil Service.

Mr. Gubbins, Financial Commissioner; Mr. Om-
manney, Judicial Commissioner, killed; Mr. Cooper,
Secretary, Chief Commissioner; Mr. Martin, Deputy-
Commissioner, Lucknow; Mr. Benson, Deputy-Commis-
sioner, Durriabad; Mr. Capper, Deputy-Commissioner,
Mullaon; Mr. Lawrence, Officiating Deputy-Commis-
sioner, Gondah, wounded, recovered; Mr. Thornhill,
Assistant-Commissioner, Lucknow, slightly wounded,

recovered — dangerously wounded, since dead ; Mr. Boulderson, Assistant-Commissioner, Lucknow, slightly wounded, recovered.

Ladies and Children in Garrison.

Mrs. Hayes and child, Mr. Edgell and child, Mrs. Marriot, Mrs. Inglis and three children, Mrs. Barwell and child, Mrs. Thomas and child (Mrs. Thomas, dead), Mrs. Lewin and two children, Mrs. Staples, Mrs. Radcliffe and three children (one child dead), Mrs. Boileau and three children, Mrs. Case and sister, Mrs. Steeven, Mrs. Giddings, Mrs. Bruere and four children, Mrs. Germon, Mrs. Aitken, Mrs. Pitt and child, Mrs. Apthorp and child (child dead), Mrs. Darrah and two children, Miss Palmer killed, Mrs. Bird and two children (one child dead), Mrs. Green (dead), Mrs. Huxham and two children (one child dead). Mrs. Ouseley and three children (two children dead), Mrs. Dashwood and three children (one child dead), Mrs. Wells and child, Mrs. Halford, Miss Halford, Mrs. Strangways and four children (one child dead), Mrs. Brydon and two children, Mrs. Stuart and child, Mrs. Banks and child, Mrs. Birch, Mrs. Orr and child, Mrs. Hearsey, Mrs. Barlow, Mrs. Forbes and three children (two children dead), Mrs. Graham and two children (one child dead), Mrs. Gall, Mrs. Barbor, Mrs. Clarke, Mrs. Soppitt, Mrs. Grant and child (both dead), Mrs. Watson and child, Mrs. Harris, Mrs. Polehampton, Mrs. Ogilvie,

Mrs. Fayrer and child, Mrs. Gubbins, Miss Nepean, Mrs. Ommaney, two Misses Ommaney, Mrs. Couper and three children, Mrs. Martin and two children (two children dead), Mrs. Benson and child (child dead), Mrs. Thornhill and child (child dead), Mrs. Schilling, Mrs. Hale and child, (both dead), Mrs. Fullerton and child (child dead), Mrs. Dorin, killed; Mrs Kendall and child (child dead), Mrs. Bartrum and child (child dead), Mrs. Clarke and child (both dead), Mrs. Anderson and child (both dead), Mrs. Anderson, Dr. Mrs. Boileau and four children (one child dead), Miss E. E. Birch.

European Women and Children in Garrison.

Mrs. Evans, dead; Mrs. Brett and child (child dead), Mrs. Ball and child; Mrs. Cane and three children; Mrs. Court and two children; Mrs. Connell and child; Mrs. Grant; Mrs. Abbott and child (child dead); Mrs. Hembro and three children; Mrs. Purcell and child; Mrs. Longton and child; Mrs. Morgan; Mrs. Sexton; Mrs. Ramsay; Mrs. Watson and child; Mrs. Ryder; Mrs. Wells and child; Mrs. Woods and three children (one child dead); Mrs. Morton and child (child dead); Mrs. Baxter and three children; Mrs. Fitzgerald and child; Mrs. Fitzgerald and three children (one child dead); Mrs. Martin; Mrs. Kinsley and four children; Mrs. Rae; Mrs. Gabriell and three children; Mrs. Pew, senior; Mrs. Pew, junior, and four children (two children dead); Mrs. Ireland and child; Mrs. Swarris and three children; Mrs. Gambooa; Mrs. Blyth and child (child dead); Mrs. Jones; Mrs. Luxted; Miss Luxted; Mrs. Catania; Mrs. Forbes; Mrs. Blaney; Mrs. Hyde and two children; Mrs. Sequera, senior; Mrs. Sequera, junior, killed; Mrs. Chrestien; Miss Sequera, Mrs. Vaughan and two children; Mrs. Beale; Mrs. Hardingham; Mrs. Sinclair; Miss Hampton; Mrs. Elliott; Mrs. Sangster and two children; Mrs. Barnett and child; Miss Sangster; Mrs. Browne; Mrs. Hamilton and three children (two children dead); Mrs. Velozo; Miss Velozo; Mrs. Horn and three children; Mrs. Parry and four children; Mrs. Ereth; Mrs. Bates; Mrs. Scott and child (child dead); Mrs. Need and three children; Mrs. Higgins, dead; Mrs. Williams and child (child dead); Mrs. Wilkinson, dead; Mrs. Allnutt and child (child dead); Mrs. Reilly and child (child dead); Mrs. Collins and child (both dead); Mrs. Macgrenan; Mrs. Garland and child; Miss Clarke; Mrs. J. J. Phillips; Mrs. W. Phillips and child; Mrs. Leslie; Mrs. Lincoln and child; Mrs. Chick and two children (one child dead); Mrs. Clancey and two children; Mrs. Joyce and child; Mrs. Best and child (child dead); Mrs. Pidgeon; Mrs. Todd and child; Mrs. Blunt; Mrs. Garrett and two children; Mrs. Pedron; Miss Marshall; Miss Savaille; Miss Campagnac; Mrs. Dudman and three children (two children dead); Mrs. Ward and child; Mrs. Dudman 2nd, Mrs. Rennick; Mrs.

Derozario; Mrs. Dacosta; Mrs. Archer and two children; Mrs. Hilton and two children; Mrs. Dera Vara and two children; Mrs. Pender and four children; Mrs. McDonnough and two children; Mrs. Oliver and two children; Mrs. Brown; Mrs. Rontleff and child; Mrs. Curwan and child; Mrs. Lynch and child; Mrs. Moreton and two children (both children dead); Mrs. Smith and three children; Mrs. Brandoff; Mrs. Curtain and three children; Mrs. Kennedy; Mrs. Bally and two children; Mrs. Peter; Miss Kennedy; Mrs. Burnet and child; Mrs. Cook and four children (one child dead); Mrs. Bryson and four children (one child dead); Mrs. Marshall; Mrs. Rutledge and two children; Mrs. Lawrence and two children; (one child dead); Mrs. Samson; Mrs. Horan and three children; Mrs. Kavanagh and four children (one child dead); Mrs. F. Marshall and two children; Mrs. Sago; Mrs. Virtue; Miss Virtue; Miss Brown; Mrs. F. Williams and two children; Mrs. Gordon and two children; Mrs. Hoff; Mrs. Wittenbaker and eight children; Mrs. Donnithorne and two children (one child dead); Mrs. Pearce and two children; Mrs. Mendes, dead; Miss Gardner; Miss Roberts; Mrs. Dubois, senior; Mrs. Dubois, junior; Mrs. Campagnac, senior; Mrs. Campagnac, junior, and four children; Miss Campagnac, 1st; Miss Campagnac, 2nd; Mrs. Mahar and two children; Mrs. Twitchem; Mrs. Marley and one child; Miss Hampton; Mrs. Longden; Miss Rodgers; Mrs. Duff and child; Mrs.

Griffiths and three children ; Mrs. Keogh and five children (three children dead) ; Mrs. Molloy and five children;
Mrs. Hernon and four children ; Mrs. Bickers and three
children; Mrs. Barrett and three children (one child
dead); Mrs. Casey and five children (one child dead);
Mrs. Alone, Miss Alone; Miss Arno ; Miss Robinson;
Miss Bowhear ; Mrs. Johannes and child; Mrs. Queiros
and child ; Mrs. Dias ; Mrs. Pelling ; Mrs. Nazareth and
two children (Mrs. Nazareth, dead) ; Mrs. Nugent, junior,
and three children ; Mrs. Joseph and three children ;
Mrs. Hamilton ; Mrs. Blenman ; Mrs. Bates and child ;
Mrs. Barfoot.

Members of the Uncovenanted Service.

Messrs. J. F. Macgrenan, R. Garland, W. E. Fitzgerald,
R. M. Collins, F. Leach, F. Williams, F. Knight, J. Gor-
don, E. Hoff, R. Dorrett, Anthony Wharton, Wittenbaker,
Wittenbaker, junior (killed), S. Williams, Donnithorne,
Velozo, Pearce, Mendes (killed), Phillips, French, Leslie,
Lincoln, Chick, W. Phillips, Clancey (killed), Ewart,
Todd, R. Joyce, Thriepland Blund, Forrester (wounded),
Potter, Kavanagh, Marshall, Forder, May, Martin, Mor-
gan (wounded), McRae (wounded), Bryson (killed), J.
Brown (killed), C. Brown (killed), O. Browne (dead),
W. Marshall (killed), E. Sequera (killed), Blancey
(wounded, recovered), Rutledge (wounded, recovered),
Duhan, Hutton, Owen, Morgan, Lawrence, Sarle, Sequera,
Parey, Allnutt, B. Alone, A. Alone (wounded), A. Bates,

Blenham (wounded), Bailey (wounded, recovered),
Bickers (wounded), Ereth (killed), T. Catania, C.
Catania, Hardingham, Rees, J. Sinclair (wounded),
McAuliffe (killed), Sinclair (pensioner), Rae, Gabriel,
Samuels, Pew, sen., A. Pew, jun., G. Ireland, W.
Ireland, Swarries (wounded, recovered), Fernandes,
Blythe, Jones, Luxted (pensioner), Hyde (wounded,
slightly recovered), Howard, Forbes, Blaney, Deprat,
(killed), W. Hamilton, Sequera, Sequera, jun. (wounded,
recovered), Chrestien, Schmidth (wounded, since dead),
Collins, Vaughan (wounded, recovered) Elliott, Sangster,
Beale (killed), Queiros, Queiros, junior, Queiros 3rd,
Johannes, Nazareth, Dias, Signor Barsotelli, Jeoffry, W.
Brown, Mitchell, Johnson, Symes, Wells (killed), Dubois,
Campagnac, C. Campagnac, E. Dudman, Owen, Hill,
Crabb (killed), Need (killed), Ward, Barry, Casey
(dead), Barrett (dead), Wiltshire (dead), Macmanus
(killed), Cameron (dead), Gerald Cameron (merchant),
H. H. Birch (son of the late Lieut.-Col. F. W. Birch).

Martiniere School.

Mr. Schilling, Principal; Mr. Crank, Assistant; Messrs.
Archer, Dodd, Wall, Hilton, Dera Vara, De Verrine, and
boys.

THE END.

www.ingramcontent.com/pod-product-compliance
Lightning Source LLC
Chambersburg PA
CBHW030934150426
42812CB00064B/2843/J

* 9 7 8 1 8 4 7 3 4 5 4 4 8 *